oxymoronica

Also by Dr. Mardy Grothe

Never Let a Fool Kiss You or a Kiss Fool You

oxymoronica

PARADOXICAL WIT AND WISDOM
FROM HISTORY'S GREATEST WORDSMITHS

By Dr. Mardy Grothe

HarperResource
An Imprint of HarperCollins*Publishers*

HarperCollins books may be purchased for educational, business,
or sales promotional use. For information, please write:
Special Markets Department, HarperCollins Publishers Inc.,
10 East 53rd Street, New York, NY 10022.

FIRST EDITION

Designed by Mary Austin Speaker

Library of Congress Cataloging-in-Publication Data

Grothe, Mardy.
   Oxymoronica : paradoxical wit and wisdom from history's
greatest wordsmiths / by Mardy Grothe.
      p. cm.
   Includes index.
   ISBN 0-06-053699-3
      1. Quotations, English. 2. Oxymoron. I. Title.

PN6081.G77 2004
082—dc22

                                             2003056646

08 WBC/RRD 20 19 18 17

table of contents

foreword

by
Richard Lederer

My son, Howard, and daughter, Annie, are full-time professional poker players who live and move and have their beings in that windowless, clockless pleasure dome known as Las Vegas. It's an easy life—earning thousands of dollars in a single night just sitting around playing card games. But it's a hard-knock life, too, what with the long, sedentary hours; the addictive behavior and secondhand smoke that suffuse the poker rooms; and the times when Lady Luck goes out whoring and your pocketbook and ego get roughed up.

How best to catch and crystallize this collide-o-scopic life my children lead, this life of gorgeous poker rooms and hearts of darkness, of Euclidean clarity and survival of the meanest? Bob "Silver Eagle" Thompson, tournament director of the World Series of Poker at Binion's Horseshoe casino, said it best: "Poker is a tough way to make an easy living."

That's a paradox, a statement that seems absurd or self-contradictory but that, as Mardy Grothe illuminates in what you are about to read, turns out to be true. Paradox is a particularly powerful device to ensnare truth because it concisely illuminates the contradictions that are at the very heart of our lives. It engages our hearts and minds because, beyond its figurative employment, paradox has always been at the center of the human condition. "Man's real life," wrote Carl Jung, "consists of a complex of inexorable opposites—day and night, birth and death, happiness and misery, good and evil. If it were not so, existence would come to an end."

Paradox was a fact of life long before it became a literary and rhetorical device. Who among us has not experienced something ugly in everything beautiful, something true in everything false, something female in everything male, or, as King Claudius says in Shakespeare's *Hamlet*, "mirth in funeral" and "dirge in marriage"?

What you are about to read is the quintessential collection of memorable, push-me-pull-you, *yin-yang* statements. Mardy Grothe has labored lovingly in the word yards of paradoxology to show us that we are, to borrow two lines from Alexander Pope's "Essay on Man,"

Sole judge of Truth, in endless Error hurled:
The glory, jest, and riddle of the world!

As you—glory, jest, and riddle—feast on the wise and witty examples and explanations in *Oxymoronica,* you will discover truths about your life that you did not know you knew.

oxymoronica

an introduction to oxymoronica

O xymoronica?" you might be thinking, "What's that?" While you surely know what an *oxymoron* is, *oxymoronica* is probably a new word to you. You won't find it in any dictionary (at least not yet) because I came up with it only a few years ago. In coining *oxymoronica*, I was inspired by words you may know:

Erotica. Literature or art that is intended to arouse sexual desire.
Exotica. Things that are curiously unusual or excitingly strange.

Playing off these words, I use the word *oxymoronica* to describe quotations that contain incompatible or incongruous elements. Many examples of *oxymoronica* appear illogical or self-contradictory on the surface. But at a deeper level, they usually make a great deal of sense and are often profoundly true.

When people are asked to describe an *oxymoron*, they almost always think of a "contradiction in terms" like *jumbo shrimp, acting naturally, pretty ugly*, or, according to some, *military intelligence*. Sometimes an oxymoron is neatly inserted into an observation, as when the actor Alec Guinness observed:

Acting is happy agony.

"Happy" and "agony" are contradictory emotional states that simply don't go together, but Guinness links them in a way that captures one of the most important characteristics of the acting profession. It's a perfect oxymoronic observation—false at a superficial level, true at a deeper one.

The same may be said about a famous line from the actress Ava Gardner:

I am deeply superficial.

In normal discourse, "deep" is the opposite of superficial. But when Gardner links these two antonyms together, the marriage of opposites arrests our attention and tantalizes our thinking. The Polish writer Stanislaw Lec was thinking along the same lines when he once said of a peer:

Even his ignorance is encyclopedic.

Lec was describing someone whose ignorance was so immense he could have called it "vast." But he chose to call it "encyclopedic," adding more pizzazz to his remark.

Another example occurs in the Albert Camus observation:

I love my country too much to be a nationalist.

Camus is suggesting that an extreme love for one's country—which often goes by the name *nationalism*—is not a good thing. His point is that he wouldn't want to do something so detrimental to a country he loves.

All of these quotes contain a juxtaposition of opposing terms. They may be described by the adjective *oxymoronic* because they are characterized by or related to the rhetorical figure called an *oxymoron*. The Oxford English Dictionary defines *oxymoron* this way:

> *A rhetorical figure by which contradictory or incongruous terms are conjoined so as to give point to the statement or expression; an expression in its superficial or literal meaning self-contradictory or absurd, but involving a point.*

The word, which appears in English for the first time in 1640, has an interesting etymology. In ancient Greek *oxus* means "sharp or pointed" and *moros* means "dull, stupid, or foolish." So *oxymoron* is itself an oxymoron, literally meaning "a sharp dullness" or "pointed foolishness." Technically, the correct plural form of the word is *oxymora*, but so many people say *oxymorons* that (except for purists, pedants, and yours truly) it is now generally regarded as an acceptable usage.

The best examples of *oxymoronica* don't contain a simple *contradiction in terms;* they contain what might be described as a *contradiction in ideas.* Many oxymoronic observations stretch our minds and expand our thinking:

Free love is too expensive.

BERNADETTE DEVLIN

Chivalry is the most delicate form of contempt.

ALBERT GUERARD

Melancholy is the pleasure of being sad.

VICTOR HUGO

The superfluous is the most necessary.

VOLTAIRE

Observations like these are usually called *paradoxical*, and all are consistent with one of the definitions of the word *paradox:*

> *A statement that seems self-contradictory, false, or absurd but is nonetheless well-founded or true.*

The word shows up for the first time in English in 1540, a hundred years before the appearance of the word *oxymoron*. *Paradox* also comes from two ancient Greek words, *para* meaning "beyond" and *doxa* meaning "opinion." Literally, it means "beyond opinion," but it originally conveyed the sense of "being beyond the pale of current opinion" or "contrary to current thinking." In the early days, it had a negative connotation, suggesting something that was fantastically unbelievable or even heretical. Shakespeare used the word in this sense when he wrote in *Othello*, "These are old fond paradoxes to make fools laugh i' the alehouse." Over time, the word gradually took on today's more favorable connotation—something that is true even though it may look false.

Many famous sayings in history fit under the umbrella of oxymoronica:

Less is more.

Coined by Robert Browning and popularized by the German-born American architect Ludwig Mies van der Rohe, nothing could be further from the literal truth. But when people use this expression, they're not speaking logically, they're using self-contradictory phrasing to describe an important principle—keeping things simple and avoiding unnecessary detail often improves things. Yes, one could say "Simpler is better," but such a bland observation wouldn't attract our attention like Browning's more provocative observation.

To grasp the meaning of oxymoronic and paradoxical observations, people must be able to engage in abstract thinking. If you ask a group of early-elementary-school students, "What does *less is more* mean?," most of them won't know because they're at an age when people tend to think concretely. Ask them the same question a few years later and the percentage of those answering correctly will shoot up. Another famous example comes from the French writer Alphonse Karr:

The more things change, the more they remain the same.

This observation is so popular that people often refer to it as an "old saying" or a "French proverb," failing to credit Karr as the author. At a literal level, the statement is false—things that change are clearly not the same. But at another level, Karr is describing one of life's most important lessons: Even though many things change dramatically as the years go by, essential aspects of the human condition remain remarkably similar over time.

Some examples of oxymoronica are ancient. More than twenty-five hundred years ago, the Chinese sage Lao-Tzu wrote:

To lead the people, walk behind them.

Lao-Tzu is revealing an ancient secret about leadership with these words. To forge a strong connection between leaders and followers, he is suggesting, the people must feel as if their leaders are truly "behind them." That is, the people must believe that their leaders will be helpful to them as they strive to achieve their most important life goals.

A paradoxical quote that I discovered many years ago took on renewed meaning after the attacks on the World Trade Center and Pentagon on September 11, 2001:

> **A nation is only at peace when it's at war.**
>
> HUGH KINGSMILL

How can a nation be at peace when it's at war? Kingsmill's point is that a nation experiences the highest levels of domestic peace when it is united against a common enemy. The day before September 11, there were deep divisions within the United States. The day after, the country was united in ways that hadn't been seen since World War II.

An oxymoron has been wisely described as "a compressed paradox." Looking at it the other way around, I think of a paradox as "an extended oxymoron." To me, they're close cousins because they both link up contradictory or incongruous elements. And they both play around in the most fascinating way with the difference between literal truth and figurative truth. For this reason, I include both oxymoronic and paradoxical observations (and a few others, as you shall soon see) under the rubric of *oxymoronica*.

Great writers have often captured the imagination of readers with inspired examples of oxymoronica. In the late 1800s, the Scottish author Robert Louis Stevenson became famous for such thrilling novels as *Treasure Island, Kidnapped,* and *The Strange Case of Dr. Jekyll and Mr. Hyde.* Among his many literary talents, Stevenson was also an acclaimed travel writer, chronicling his excursions throughout Europe and America in many articles and books. In *Across the Plains*, published in 1892, he wrote about his experiences in America, capturing the vastness of the country with a remarkable line:

We were at sea—
there is no other adequate expression—
on the plains of Nebraska.

At sea on the plains of Nebraska? The idea compels our attention. And if you've ever driven across the Great Plains in late summer—when, as far as you can see, vast acres of wheat fields roll gently with the wind—you can appreciate the truth as well as the beauty of Stevenson's observation.

Some wise person whose name has been lost to history said, "A paradox is truth standing on its head to attract our attention." This observation helps explain our long-standing fascination with statements that on the surface seem patently false or even ridiculous, but at a deeper level are profoundly true:

Perhaps the only true dignity of man
is his capacity to despise himself.

GEORGE SANTAYANA

What dignity can there be in despising oneself? In a perfect example of that old saying about a truth standing on its head to get our attention, Santayana is advancing a profound thought. Human beings have a unique capacity to reflect on their behavior. When they behave badly and then despise themselves for their not-so-honorable actions, it does seem appropriate to say they've arrived at a moment of dignity.

Another attention-grabbing observation comes from Katherine Mansfield:

If you wish to live, you must first attend your own funeral.

Since we'll all be dead when our funerals are held, Mansfield has clearly entered the paradoxical domain in this observation. After a few moments of reflection, Mansfield's meaning becomes clear. She is suggesting something many wise people have recommended over the years—that you will begin to live life fully only when you project yourself to the time of your death, imagining how you've lived your life and anticipating what will be said about you at your funeral.

Given their centuries-old interest in the Unity of Opposites (often expressed in the symbols of *yin* and *yang*), the Chinese have long appreciated self-contradictory thinking. Indeed, Lao-Tzu may have been one of the first people in history to formally recognize the deep link between truth and paradox. Writing in the sixth century B.C., he observed, "The truest sayings are paradoxical." Many of the aphorisms of China's great sages are examples.

Happiness is the absence of the striving for happiness.

CHUANG-TZU

Real knowledge is to know the extent of one's own ignorance.

CONFUCIUS

**Failure is the foundation of success . . .
success the lurking place of failure.**

LAO-TZU

Western thinkers have also been fascinated by the concept of paradoxical truth. The Danish philosopher Søren Kierkegaard once said, "The paradox is the source of the thinker's passion, and the thinker without a paradox is like a lover without feeling: a paltry mediocrity."

Henry David Thoreau, who was intimately familiar with the sayings of Confucius and the aphorisms of Lao-Tzu, put it more succinctly: "Truth is always paradoxical." Consider this example, written while Thoreau conducted his experiment in living at Walden Pond:

**I have a great deal of company in the house,
especially in the morning when nobody calls.**

When you dip below the surface of Thoreau's observation, you will soon grasp his point—he's in the best company when by himself, reading his favorite authors and reflecting on their great thoughts. A few years earlier, the English historian Edward Gibbon advanced the same idea:

I was never less alone than when by myself.

Before him, Benjamin Disraeli said pretty much the same thing:

There is a society in the deepest solitude.

And, as you'll see in more detail in a later chapter, many modern examples of oxymoronica were inspired by sentiments that go back to antiquity. In this case, the idea was first advanced by the Roman poet Albius Tibullus, who wrote in the first century B.C.:

In solitude, be a multitude to thyself.

Oxymoronic phrasing is sometimes used to express unpleasant or unpalatable truths—a situation calling for the rhetorical device of *irony*. Ironic phrasing fits perfectly under the umbrella of oxymoronica, for users of the technique say something literally that contradicts their actual meaning. In the 1920s, the American humorist Will Rogers said:

**You can't say civilization isn't advancing,
in every war they kill you in a new way.**

Clearly, finding new ways of killing people is contrary to the usual notion of how civilized societies advance, so we have a neat intermingling of opposites here. The statement is ironic in the sense that Rogers is not applauding new and improved ways of killing people, he's deploring the development. When people use irony, they say the opposite of what they mean, assuming (or at least hoping) that people will understand their true message.

A particularly biting example of ironic oxymoronica comes from the pen of the acclaimed writer and early Zionist Israel Zangwill:

> **The Jews are a frightened people.**
> **Nineteen centuries of Christian love have broken their nerves.**

A particularly clever one comes from the quirky mind and talented pen of Charles Kuralt, who wrote in his 1985 book *On the Road*:

> **Thanks to the interstate highway system, it is now possible to**
> **travel across the country from coast to coast without seeing anything.**

And if you've ever questioned the value of those seemingly interminable staff meetings at work, you'll appreciate John Kenneth Galbraith's words on the subject, first offered in his 1969 *Ambassador's Journal*:

> **Meetings are indispensable when you don't want to do anything.**

All of these observations perfectly meet the Oxford English Dictionary's definition of *irony*:

> *A figure of speech in which the intended meaning is*
> *the opposite of that expressed by the words used;*
> *usually taking the form of ridicule in which lauda-*

tory expressions are used to imply condemnation or contempt.

Exceptionally creative people—especially those in the fine arts—have always shown a special interest in self-contradictory phrasing.

> **Painting is easy when you don't know how,**
> **but very difficult when you do.**
>
> EDGAR DEGAS

> **Artists who seek perfection in everything**
> **are those who can attain it in nothing.**
>
> EUGÈNE DELACROIX

> **Every act of creation is first of all an act of destruction.**
>
> PABLO PICASSO

> **The truest poetry is the most feigning.**
>
> WILLIAM SHAKESPEARE

History's great wits and wordsmiths have also been fascinated by this powerful method of presenting thoughts and ideas. Benjamin Disraeli, one of the wittiest and most eloquent politicians in world history, once said:

> **Like all great travelers,**
> **I have seen more than I remember,**
> **and remember more than I have seen.**

Savvy readers will recognize this as an example of *chiasmus* (ky-AZ-mus), another one of my favorite literary devices. In chiasmus, there's a reversal in the order of words in two parallel phrases (for more, go to www.chiasmus.com). The Disraeli observation is also a neat exam-

. Notice how the final line describes a logical
an we remember something we've never seen? In
eli is describing the all-too-common tendency for
embellish things when they recount their experi-
ick home. Mark Twain, a fan of Disraeli's, was
this observation when he wrote:

> **When I was younger, I could remember anything,**
> **whether it happened or not,**
> **but I am getting old, and soon I shall remember only the latter.**

Oscar Wilde may also have been inspired by Disraeli when he wrote:

> **Memory is the diary that chronicles things that never have happened**
> **and couldn't possibly have happened.**

Some of our best modern humorists have also enjoyed playing the
oxymoronic game, writing things that seem nonsensical at first but
brilliant upon reflection:

> **I don't drink. I don't like it. It makes me feel good.**
>
> OSCAR LEVANT

> **I wish people who have trouble communicating would just shut up.**
>
> TOM LEHRER

> **Why do you have to be a nonconformist like everybody else?**
>
> JAMES THURBER

Wonderful examples of oxymoronica also show up in the world of
popular culture. Notice how the following cultural icons have used

the device to capture important aspects of their lives and their work:

> **It's kind of fun to do the impossible.**
>
> WALT DISNEY

> **People want economy and they will pay any price to get it.**
>
> LEE IACOCCA

> **You'd be surprised how much it costs to look this cheap.**
>
> DOLLY PARTON

> **If I say, "Oh nice," about seven times in the same show, things aren't going well.**
>
> OPRAH WINFREY

No figure of speech or literary device can be considered fully worth its salt until it proves useful in one of the most popular of human activities—putting people down, or at least putting them in their place. In this arena, oxymoronica has few rivals. After Doris Day achieved enormous popularity for her squeaky-clean, girl-next-door image in all those 1950s and 1960s movies with Rock Hudson, Oscar Levant put it all into perspective when he observed about the actress:

> **I knew her before she was a virgin.**

Predictably, oxymoronic insults have also been hurled with vigor in the political arena. In the 1980s, James "Scotty" Reston of the *New York Times* described Ronald Reagan as:

> **An authentic phony.**

And Theodore Roosevelt once said of the tenth U.S. president, John Tyler:

> **He has been called a mediocre man; but this is unwarranted flattery.**
> **He was a politician of monumental littleness.**

Let me bring this introductory chapter to a close by mentioning a fascinating variation on the theme—self-contradictory phrasing that comes about by accident. Two of the best examples of "inadvertent oxymoronica" come from two of the most colorful figures in American history:

> **A verbal contract isn't worth the paper it's printed on.**
> SAMUEL GOLDWYN

> **Nobody goes there anymore. It's too crowded.**
> YOGI BERRA, ON A POPULAR RESTAURANT

I've presented about three dozen quotes in this chapter. As you shall shortly see, I've only skimmed the surface. In the remainder of the book, I'll present about fourteen hundred oxymoronic and paradoxical quotations, all culled from my private collection, which now numbers between eight and ten thousand. Despite the enormous number of such quotes in existence, I've never seen them singled out and presented in a quotation anthology. That will change with this book.

In this introduction, I've tried my best to whet your interest. The rest of the book is divided into chapters like "Oxymoronic Wit & Humor," "Political Oxymoronica," "Ancient Oxymoronica," and "Oxymoronic Insults." In each chapter, I'll introduce the subject in a way that I hope you'll find interesting. Then I'll present several dozen quotes that fit into the theme. Within each chapter, I'll arrange the quotations alphabetically by author. If you wish to locate quotes from a particular person, consult the author index at the back of the book.

This book is for language-loving readers who get a kick out of seeing words and expressions used in clever or creative ways—what is commonly called *wordplay*. It's also designed for intellectually oriented readers who enjoy playing around with thoughts and ideas. These are people who get a special pleasure out of seeing things from unusual perspectives—what might be called *ideaplay*.

The book may also appeal to readers with a professional interest in language and ideas: writers and poets; public speakers; speechwriters; preachers; and, of course, teachers and professors—especially those who teach writing, poetry, philosophy, and public speaking.

As you delve into the book, my best advice is to *go slowly*. You're about to encounter a host of thought-provoking, mind-stretching, perception-altering quotations. These are quotations that deserve to be mulled over and thought through, not skimmed over quickly. One of my advance readers said he closed his eyes for a moment after reading each quote. A chocoholic, he likened his reading experience to eating high-quality candy. He wanted to savor each quote.

As for me, I've been a practicing psychologist for more than twenty-five years. In addition to my professional pursuits, I've had a lifelong love affair with the English language. I'm a voracious reader and have been an avid quotation collector for almost forty years. After co-authoring three "business books," I ventured into the word and language arena in 1999 with *Never Let a Fool Kiss You or a Kiss Fool You*, my attempt to introduce people to the fascinating literary device of chiasmus. This is my second foray into the quotation arena, and, I hope, not my last.

While I've striven for accuracy, I'm sure I've made some mistakes. If you discover any errors or would simply like to offer some feedback, please write me in care of the publisher or e-mail me directly at: DrMGrothe@aol.com.

I've also launched a Web site where you can delve into the topic a bit deeper (and even send me some of your own favorite oxymoronic and paradoxical quotations). Come visit sometime: www.oxymoronica.com.

chapter one

OXYMORONIC WIT & HUMOR

Malcolm Muggeridge, while serving as the editor of the humor magazine *Punch,* was accused of publishing a magazine that violated standards of good taste. He defended himself and the magazine by replying:

**Good taste and humor are a contradiction in terms,
like a chaste whore.**

While much humor—especially sexual and scatological humor—is clearly of questionable taste, it's an overstatement to regard all humor as opposed to good taste. Oxymoronic humor, which is more cerebral than visceral, can be deliciously tasteful. Stand-up comics have always realized this:

Life is full of misery, loneliness, and suffering—
and it's all over much too soon.

WOODY ALLEN

We sleep in separate rooms, we have dinner apart,
we take separate vacations.
We're doing everything we can to keep our marriage together.

RODNEY DANGERFIELD

Last month I blew $5,000 on a reincarnation seminar.
I figured, hey, you only live once.

RANDY SHAKES

As you can see from these examples, oxymoronic humor is sophisticated humor. It's directed at the most important organ in the human body—the brain. The self-contradictory aspects of oxymoronic humor appeal to a special part of our mental apparatus, a part that enjoys thinking about some of life's most intriguing contradictions and paradoxes.

The world's great humorists have had a field day with oxymoronic humor:

Drawing on my fine command of language, I said nothing.

ROBERT C. BENCHLEY

One martini is all right, two is two many, three is not enough.

JAMES THURBER

The coldest winter I ever spent was a summer in San Francisco.

MARK TWAIN, ATTRIBUTED BUT NEVER VERIFIED

Our best contemporary humorists have also favored this type of humor. In 1987, Garrison Keillor decided to bring *A Prairie Home*

Companion to an end. The show had been a staple on National Public Radio for thirteen years, developing a huge audience. In 1988, broadcasting what was billed as a farewell performance from Radio City Music Hall, Keillor began the show by announcing:

It is our farewell performance, and I hope the first of many.

With many oxymoronic observations, the meaning is not immediately obvious, and sometimes the best lines can fly right over our heads. But once the meaning becomes clear, we generally admire how cleverly a point has been made or how creatively it's been expressed. Take the dread of going to the dentist. Few have expressed that common fear better than S. J. Perelman:

**As for consulting a dentist regularly,
my punctuality practically amounted to a fetish.
Every twelve years I would drop whatever I was doing
and allow wild Caucasian ponies to drag me
to a reputable orthodontist.**

The pun is another type of humor that appears to be an exception to Muggeridge's observation that humor is opposed to good taste. While some puns are sexual or risqué—and can push at the boundaries of good taste—most are simply good-natured attempts at wordplay. But if a pun is considered the lowest form of wit, as has often been said, then oxymoronic humor may be considered one of the highest. While puns—even the best of them—are often met with predictable groans, a witty oxymoronic line is often followed by an *ahhh!* of appreciation and hearty nods of approval. And every now and then, punning is combined with oxymoronic phrasing to produce a special type of hybrid observation. In his 1840 book *Up the Rhine*, English writer Thomas Hood chronicled his travels throughout Europe. Playing on the words *dam* and *damn*, he observed:

Holland . . . lies so low they're only saved by being dammed.

An important ingredient in many types of humor is the element of surprise. It's the reason we laugh at the punch line of a joke. In oxymoronic humor, the surprise comes in the unexpected marriage of concepts that are usually considered incompatible. It's the reason you probably chuckled the first time you heard expressions like *jumbo shrimp* and *military intelligence.* And it's the reason knowledgeable people derive such pleasure from lines like this one from Milton Berle:

Jews don't drink much because it interferes with their suffering.

What makes the Berle line special is the intermingling of concepts that normally don't go together—the well-known tendency of people to drown their sorrows in alcohol and the much-chronicled tendency of Jews to get a certain amount of pleasure out of life's many little afflictions, especially physical ailments. This latter phenomenon, by the way, shows up with other religious and national groups as well. The acclaimed journalist James "Scotty" Reston once wrote:

I'm a Scotch Calvinist and nothing makes us happier than misery.

English critic Leigh Hunt might have been thinking about oxymoronic humor when he wrote, "Wit is the clash and reconcilement of incongruities, the meeting of extremes around a corner." Great wits have always been predisposed to this type of humor, but none more so than the incomparable Oscar Wilde:

The suspense is terrible. I hope it will last.

Life is too important to be taken seriously.

To be natural is a very difficult pose to keep up.

Wilde and his contemporary, George Bernard Shaw, both had minds with a strong oxymoronic bent, and it is no coincidence that a popular observation about America and Britain has been attributed to both of them:

We have really everything in common with America
nowadays except, of course, language.

O.W.

England and America are two countries
separated by the same language.

G.B.S.

In these examples, Shaw was probably influenced by Wilde, since Wilde's witty lines generally came earlier and Shaw was very familiar with Wilde's work. But Shaw also crafted some highly original oxymoronic lines on his own:

I showed my appreciation of my native land in the usual Irish way:
by getting out of it as soon as I possibly could.

I believe in the discipline of silence and could talk for hours about it.

I'm an atheist and I thank God for it.

Another fascinating feature of oxymoronic wit is the appeal it has to highly intelligent people. Many of the world's most brilliant minds have loved tickling people's funny bones by exploring some of life's intriguing contradictions.

A perfect example comes from the Austrian-born English philosopher, Ludwig Wittgenstein, who once made the oxymoronic claim, "A serious work in philosophy could be written that consisted entirely of jokes." He proved his point—and delighted his associates—with this observation:

**When I came home I expected a surprise and
there was no surprise for me, so, of course, I was surprised.**

Another example comes from the Danish physicist Niels Bohr. Shortly after receiving the Nobel Prize in 1922, Bohr invited a number of reporters to his country cottage. One visitor, noticing a horseshoe hanging on the wall, teasingly asked, "Can it be that you, of all people, believe a horseshoe will bring you good luck?" Bohr replied:

**Of course not, but I understand
it brings you luck whether you believe or not.**

Why are intelligent people so fond of oxymoronic humor? It's hard to be sure, but a partial explanation may be found in the words of F. Scott Fitzgerald, who wrote, "The test of a first-rate intelligence is the ability to hold two opposed ideas in the mind at the same time, and still retain the ability to function." When opposing ideas exist in our minds, mental tension is created. But in a superior intellect, this tension is less a source of discomfort and more an opportunity to forge a new—and often witty—connection. Examples abound in the remarks of highly intelligent people:

**Science is a wonderful thing
if one does not have to earn one's living at it.**
ALBERT EINSTEIN

Always remember that you are absolutely unique.
Just like everyone else.

MARGARET MEAD

I want to die young at a ripe old age.

ASHLEY MONTAGU

There are some ideas so wrong that
only a very intelligent person could believe in them.

GEORGE ORWELL

We have to believe in free will. We've got no other choice.

ISAAC BASHEVIS SINGER

If you count yourself as a person who enjoys sophisticated humor of a mind-stretching quality, sit back, relax, and enjoy many more examples in the remainder of this chapter. As you do, recall the words of George Bernard Shaw, who once said, "When a thing is funny, search it carefully for a hidden truth."

I think people who go to a psychiatrist
ought to have their heads examined.

JANE ACE

Stay with me; I want to be alone.

JOEY ADAMS

When all else fails, read the instructions.

AGNES ALLEN

It's not that I'm afraid to die.
I just don't want to be there when it happens.

WOODY ALLEN

I'd give my right arm to be ambidextrous.

ANONYMOUS

It's easier to suffer in silence if you are sure someone is watching.

ANONYMOUS

People should be allowed to play the violin
only after they have mastered it.

ANONYMOUS

Nudists are fond of saying that when you come right down to it
everyone is alike, and, again, that
when you come right down to it everyone is different.

DIANE ARBUS

The marvelous thing about a joke with a double meaning
is that it can only mean one thing.

RONNIE BARKER

The trouble with New York is it's so convenient
to everything I can't afford.

JACK BARRY

We started off trying to set up a small anarchist community,
but people wouldn't obey the rules.

ALAN BENNETT

I'm in favor of free expression
provided it's kept rigidly under control.

ALAN BENNETT

Modesty is my best quality.

JACK BENNY

No man is so poor that he can't afford to keep one dog,
and I've seen them so poor that they could afford to keep three.

JOSH BILLINGS

I feel so miserable without you, it's almost like having you here.

STEPHEN BISHOP

If you aren't confused by quantum physics,
then you haven't really understood it.

NIELS BOHR

Prediction is very difficult, especially about the future.

NIELS BOHR

What most of us are after, when we have a picture taken,
is a good natural-looking picture that doesn't resemble us.

PEG BRACKEN

People would have more leisure time
if it weren't for all the leisure-time activities that use it up.

PEG BRACKEN

When you stop drinking, you have to deal with
this marvelous personality that started you drinking in the first place.

JIMMY BRESLIN

To appreciate nonsense requires a serious interest in life.

GELETT BURGESS

Happiness is having a large, loving, caring,
close-knit family in another city.

GEORGE BURNS

Too bad that all the people who know
how to run the country are busy
driving taxicabs and cutting hair.

GEORGE BURNS

You can't make anything idiot-proof because idiots are so ingenious.

RON BURNS

I had to give up masochism—I was enjoying it too much.

MEL CALMAN

How is it possible to have a *civil* war?

GEORGE CARLIN

There is a terrible lot of lies going about the world,
and the worst of it is that half of them are true.

WINSTON CHURCHILL

There's nothing wrong with sobriety in moderation.

JOHN CIARDI

Everybody hates me because I'm so universally liked.

PETER DE VRIES

I am a man of fixed and unbending principles,
the first of which is to be flexible at all times.

EVERETT DIRKSEN

I hate music, especially when it's played.

JIMMY DURANTE

The average tourist wants to go to places where there are no tourists.

SAM EWING

I told the doctor I was overtired, anxiety-ridden, compulsively
active, constantly depressed, with recurring fits of paranoia.
Turns out I'm normal.

JULES FEIFFER

The best cure for insomnia is to get a lot of sleep.

W. C. FIELDS

Instant gratification takes too long.

CARRIE FISHER

I feel bad that I don't feel worse.

MICHAEL FRAYN

I find nothing more depressing than optimism.

PAUL FUSSELL

Personally I know nothing about sex
because I've always been married.

ZSA ZSA GABOR

If there is a 50-50 chance that something can go wrong,
then nine times out of ten it will.

PAUL HARVEY

I wish I were either rich enough or poor enough
to do a lot of things that are impossible
in my present comfortable circumstances.

DON HEROLD

Like most native New Yorkers, I was born out of town.

HARRY HERSHFIELD

But when I don't smoke I scarcely feel as if I'm living.
I don't feel as if I'm living unless I'm killing myself.

RUSSELL HOBAN

A bank is a place that will lend you money
if you can prove that you don't need it.

BOB HOPE

Some people can stay longer in an hour than others can in a week.

WILLIAM DEAN HOWELLS

Show me a sane man
and I will cure him for you.

CARL JUNG

We are confronted by insurmountable opportunities.

WALT KELLY, FROM "POGO"

The average, healthy, well-adjusted adult
gets up at 7:30 in the morning feeling just plain terrible.

JEAN KERR

I have a terrible memory; I never forget a thing.

EDITH KONECKY

I figure you have the same chance of winning the lottery
whether you play or not.

FRAN LEBOWITZ

The fly that does not want to be swatted
is safest if it sits on the fly-swatter.

G. C. LICHTENBERG

It is difficult to keep quiet if you have nothing to say.

MALCOLM MARGOLIN

Ours is a world where people don't know what they want and are
willing to go through hell to get it.

DON MARQUIS

The secret of life is honesty and fair dealing.
If you can fake that, you've got it made.

GROUCHO MARX

There is only one thing about which I am certain,
and that is that there is very little about which one can be certain.

W. SOMERSET MAUGHAM

Our strength is often composed of the weaknesses
we're damned if we're going to show.

MIGNON MCLAUGHLIN

We'd all like a reputation for generosity
and we'd all like to buy it cheap.

MIGNON MCLAUGHLIN

I cherish the greatest respect towards everybody's
religious obligations, never mind how comical.

HERMAN MELVILLE

It infuriates me to be wrong when I know I'm right.

MOLIÈRE

There is always a right and a wrong way,
and the wrong way always seems the more reasonable.

GEORGE MOORE

If you think health care is expensive now,
wait until you see what it costs when it's free.

P. J. O'ROURKE

I have made this letter longer than usual,
because I lack the time to make it short.

BLAISE PASCAL

I now accept with equanimity the question
so constantly addressed to me,
"Are you an American?"
and merely return the accurate answer,
"Yes, I am a Canadian."

LESTER B. PEARSON

I'm often wrong, but never in doubt.

IVY BAKER PRIEST

I am not sincere, even when I say I am not.

JULES RENARD

A friend of mine, contemplating the English department:
"There are plenty of vacancies, but they're all filled."

CHRISTOPHER RICKS

Human nature is largely something that has to be overcome.

RITA RUDNER

I have come to the conclusion
after many years of sometimes sad experience
that you cannot come to any conclusions at all.

VITA SACKVILLE-WEST

I think we all have a need to know what we do not need to know.

WILLIAM SAFIRE

Wall Street indexes predicted nine out of the last five recessions.

PAUL A. SAMUELSON

I love mankind—it's people I can't stand.

CHARLES M. SCHULZ

There must be more to life than having everything.

MAURICE SENDAK

I was going to buy a copy of *The Power of Positive Thinking*,
and then I thought, "What the hell good would that do?"

RONNIE SHAKES

Thank heavens! The sun has gone in,
and I don't have to go out and enjoy it.

LOGAN PEARSALL SMITH

I hate intolerant people.

GLORIA STEINEM

Anonymity is my claim to fame.

FRED STOLLER

There is no exception to the rule that every rule has an exception.

JAMES THURBER

I like a view but I like to sit with my back turned to it.

ALICE B. TOKLAS

Health food makes me sick.

CALVIN TRILLIN

I have never let my schooling interfere with my education.

MARK TWAIN

Few things are harder to put up with
than the annoyance of a good example.

MARK TWAIN

Nothing is more irritating than not being invited to a party
you wouldn't be seen dead at.

BILL VAUGHAN

If there is anything the nonconformist hates worse than a conformist,
it's another nonconformist who doesn't
conform to the prevailing standard of nonconformity.

BILL VAUGHAN

Let us all be happy, and live within our means,
even if we have to borrow the money to do it with.

ARTEMUS WARD

It is a folly to expect men to do all that
they may be reasonably expected to do.

RICHARD WHATELY

I yield to no one in my admiration for the office as a social center,
but it's no place actually to get any work done.

KATHERINE WHITEHORN

The Jews and Arabs should settle their dispute
in the true spirit of Christian charity.

ALEXANDER WILEY

chapter two

THE HUMAN CONDITION

In his 1830 *Lectures on the Philosophy of World History*, the German philosopher Georg Hegel said:

We learn from history that we do not learn from history.

Hegel's point was not particularly profound. Nor was it highly original. He was essentially repeating something many others before him had said—human beings keep repeating the mistakes of their ancestors. But his way of describing the problem went on to become one of the most widely quoted observations of all time. That's the way it is with great oxymoronic quotes. Yes, they compress much wisdom into a few words. But more important, they package those words so cleverly that the observations often become classics. Hegel's observation inspired other great thinkers to say virtually the same thing:

That men do not learn very much from the lessons of history
is the most important of all the lessons that history has to teach.

ALDOUS HUXLEY

We learn from experience that men
never learn anything from experience.

GEORGE BERNARD SHAW

Even though it's true that people often forget the lessons of the past, it's also true that thoughtful observers have learned enough from history to make some pretty truthful generalizations about the human condition. Some of the best have taken an oxymoronic form:

The significance of man is that
he is insignificant and is aware of it.

CARL BECKER

The most incomprehensible thing about the world
is that it is comprehensible.

ALBERT EINSTEIN

It seems fitting that some of the most penetrating observations about the human condition take the form of oxymoronic reflections about *life* itself:

A life of ease is a difficult pursuit.

WILLIAM COWPER

Life begins when a person first realizes how soon it ends.

MARCELENE COX

It is only by knowing how little life has in store for us
that we are able to look on the bright side and avoid disappointment.

ELLEN GLASGOW

Life is easier than you'd think; all that is necessary is
to accept the impossible, do without the indispensable,
and bear the intolerable.

KATHLEEN NORRIS

Life begins on the other side of despair.

JEAN-PAUL SARTRE

Many oxymoronic observations turn conventional ideas on their heads. For example, it's almost universally agreed that achieving goals—especially lofty goals—leads to a feeling of triumph and accomplishment. That is often true. But not always. Sometimes, achieving goals can lead to feelings of emptiness, depression, or even despair. A number of people have noted this fascinating aspect of the human experience:

To have realized your dream makes you feel lost.

ORIANA FALLACI

From the satisfaction of desire there may arise, accompanying joy and
as it were sheltering behind it, something not unlike despair.

ANDRÉ GIDE

If there is nothing left to desire, there is everything to fear,
an unhappy state of happiness.

BALTASAR GRACIÁN

Need and struggle are what excite and inspire us;
our hour of triumph is what brings the void.

WILLIAM JAMES

Another cherished assumption has to do with the principle of discussing things fully before embarking on a course of action. Most would agree that this is a good idea. And it usually is. But sometimes we can talk so much that we engage in the intricacies of overplanning, going down blind alleys and inadvertently setting traps for ourselves. An example comes from Leon Trotsky's 1935 *Diary in Exile*. A leader of the Russian revolution, Trotsky was booted out of his homeland by Stalin after Lenin's death. He continued his anti-Stalinist activities from a number of Western countries, eventually paying for his agitation by being assassinated in Mexico on Stalin's orders. While in exile, he also began writing about his life, once reflecting:

If we had more time for discussion
we should probably have made a great many more mistakes.

Trotsky, even though best known for his political activities, was also a pretty fair thinker and writer. In another observation from his memoirs, he wrote:

Old age is the most unexpected of all the things
that can happen to a man.

How can something we fully expect come as a surprise? One reason, in this particular instance, is that old age sneaks up so stealthily, descending on us years before we're ready for it. Another reason is more general and goes to the heart of the human psyche. What we have long expected to happen, when it finally does arrive, rarely looks like what we imagined. Mark Twain, ever the keen observer of the human scene, described it well:

> **A thing long expected takes the form**
> **of the unexpected when at last it comes.**

More recently, James Michener wrote on the same subject:

> **We are never prepared for what we expect.**

Many aspects of the human experience fall quite naturally into the paradoxical domain. And, fortunately, writers throughout history have been happy to draw these paradoxical realities to our attention. One of the most fascinating is embedded in a quote from the French essayist Montaigne:

> **Nothing fixes a thing so intensely in the memory**
> **as the wish to forget it.**

What Montaigne is pointing out is something that has frustrated many people over the centuries—consciously attempting to do something is often one of the worst ways of achieving a goal. To make matters worse, it sometimes even produces the opposite result. This kind of thing shows up in a variety of different ways in human life:

> **The truth that many people never understand, until it is too late,**
> **is that the more you try to avoid suffering the more you suffer.**
>
> THOMAS MERTON

> **As a rule, for no one does life drag more disagreeably**
> **than for him who tries to speed it up.**
>
> JEAN PAUL RICHTER

Change really becomes a necessity when we try not to do it.

ANNE WILSON SCHAEF

The ladies who try to keep their beauty are the ladies who lose it.

LOGAN PEARSALL SMITH

Another interesting human dynamic has been known for centuries, but was particularly well stated by the economist and philosopher Kenneth E. Boulding:

We must always be on the lookout for perverse dynamic processes
which carry even good things to excess.
It is precisely these excesses which become the most evil things. . . .
The devil, after all, is a fallen angel.

The problem Boulding is describing is one of the oldest oxymoronic themes in history—that too much of a good thing is bad. It's been chronicled in a variety of different ways by a number of different people over the centuries:

You do not know what life means
when all the difficulties are removed!
I am simply smothered and sickened with advantages.
It is like eating a sweet dessert the first thing in the morning.

JANE ADDAMS

To spend too much time in studies is sloth.

FRANCIS BACON

The most exquisite folly is made of wisdom spun too fine.

BENJAMIN FRANKLIN

> **It is not good to have too much liberty.**
> **It is not good to have all one wants.**
>
> BLAISE PASCAL

As you shall see a number of times in this book, the earliest statement of many oxymoronic themes goes back to the earliest days of civilization. That's certainly true in this case. In the fifth century B.C., Sophocles wrote in *Electra:*

> **There is a point beyond which even justice becomes unjust.**

And writing on the other side of the world in the fourth century B.C., the Chinese scholar Chuang-Tzu put it this way:

> **To have enough is good luck, to have more than enough is harmful.**
> **This is true of all things, but especially of money.**

In the rest of this chapter, let's continue our look at oxymoronic observations on various aspects of the human condition. As you proceed, notice how often this collection of highly divergent quotes helps you see some old realities in some fresh new ways.

> **Our real blessings often appear to us**
> **in the shape of pains, losses and disappointments.**
>
> JOSEPH ADDISON

> **Found a Society of Honest Men, and all the thieves will join it.**
>
> ALAIN (EMILE CHARTIER)

> **The paradox of reality is that no image is as compelling**
> **as the one which exists only in the mind's eye.**
>
> SHANA ALEXANDER

The man with a host of friends
who slaps on the back everybody he meets
is regarded as the friend of nobody.

ARISTOTLE (FOURTH CENTURY B.C.)

The most melancholy of human reflections, perhaps,
is that, on the whole, it is a question whether
the benevolence of mankind does more good or harm.

WALTER BAGEHOT

The cannon thunders . . . limbs fly in all directions . . .
one can hear the groans of victims
and the howling of those performing the sacrifice . . .
it's Humanity in search of happiness.

CHARLES BAUDELAIRE

There is in the human race some dark spirit of recalcitrance,
always pulling us in the direction contrary
to that in which we are reasonably expected to go.

MAX BEERBOHM

There are people so addicted to exaggeration
that they can't tell the truth without lying.

JOSH BILLINGS

You never know what is enough
unless you know what is more than enough.

WILLIAM BLAKE

It is easier to forgive an Enemy than to forgive a Friend.

WILLIAM BLAKE

They that endeavor to abolish vice, destroy also virtue;
for contraries, though they destroy one another,
are yet the life of one another.

SIR THOMAS BROWNE

All men that are ruined,
are ruined on the side of their natural propensities.

EDMUND BURKE

We have three kinds of friends: those who love us,
those who are indifferent to us, and those who hate us.

NICOLAS CHAMFORT

The final delusion is the belief that one has lost all delusions.

MAURICE CHAPELAIN

The secret of success in life is known only
to those who have not succeeded.

JOHN CHURTON COLLINS

We are sure to be losers when we quarrel with ourselves;
it is a civil war, and in all such contentions, triumphs are defeats.

CHARLES CALEB COLTON

Some who profess to despise all flattery are nevertheless
to be flattered by being told that they do despise it.

CHARLES CALEB COLTON

The world is full of people whose notion of a satisfactory future is,
in fact, a return to the idealized past.

ROBERTSON DAVIES

It's usually the most wounded among us who inflict pain on others.

PATTI DAVIS

We always weaken whatever we exaggerate.

JEAN-FRANÇOIS DE LA HARPE

The ever-alert, the conscientiously wakeful—
how many fine things they fail to see.

NORMAN DOUGLAS

We know nothing about motivation.
All we can do is write books about it.

PETER DRUCKER

Civilizations commonly die from the excessive development
of certain characteristics which had at first
contributed to their success.

RENÉ DUBOS

Th' fav'rite pastime iv civilized man is croolty to other civilized man.

FINLEY PETER DUNNE

The efforts which we make to escape from our destiny
only serve to lead us into it.

RALPH WALDO EMERSON

The end of the human race will be that
it will eventually die of civilization.

RALPH WALDO EMERSON

The means by which certain pleasures are gained
bring pains many times greater than the pleasures.

EPICURUS (THIRD CENTURY B.C.)

Experience teaches you that the man who looks you straight in the eye,
particularly if he adds a firm handshake, is hiding something.

CLIFTON FADIMAN

The average man, who does not know what to do with this life,
wants another one which shall last forever.

ANATOLE FRANCE

Success has ruin'd many a man.

BENJAMIN FRANKLIN

Many a man thinks he is buying pleasure,
when he is really selling himself a slave to it.

BENJAMIN FRANKLIN

When people are least sure they are most dogmatic.

JOHN KENNETH GALBRAITH

A person who is going to commit an inhuman act
invariably excuses himself by saying, "I'm only human, after all."

SYDNEY J. HARRIS

Our dilemma is that we hate change and love it at the same time;
what we really want is for things to remain the same but get better.

SYDNEY J. HARRIS

We never do anything well 'till we
cease to think about the manner of doing it.

WILLIAM HAZLITT

Lonely people talking to each other can make each other lonelier.

LILLIAN HELLMAN

When people are free to do as they please,
they usually imitate each other.

ERIC HOFFER

It is a perplexing and unpleasant truth that when men
have something worth fighting for, they do not feel like fighting.

ERIC HOFFER

The hardest thing is writing a recommendation for someone we know.

KIN HUBBARD

For prying into any human affairs,
none are equal to those whom it does not concern.

VICTOR HUGO

A permanent state of transition is man's most noble condition.

JUAN RAMÓN JIMÉNEZ

The vanity of being known to be trusted with a secret
is generally one of the chief motives to disclose it.

SAMUEL JOHNSON

How many weak shoulders have craved heavy burdens!

JOSEPH JOUBERT

Man needs difficulties;
they are necessary for health.

CARL JUNG

The more immoral we become in big ways,
the more puritanical we become in little ways.

FLORENCE KING

There are times when lying is the most sacred of duties.

EUGENE LABICHE

Only in growth, reform, and change, paradoxically enough,
is true security to be found.

ANNE MORROW LINDBERGH

The richer your friends, the more they will cost you.

ELISABETH MARBURY

It has amazed me that the most incongruous traits should exist in
the same person and, for all that, yield a plausible harmony.

W. SOMERSET MAUGHAM

A learned fool is more foolish than an ignorant one.

MOLIÈRE

A man that is ashamed of passions that are natural and reasonable
is generally proud of those that are shameful and silly.

MARY WORTLEY MONTAGU

I have seen people rude by being over-polite.

MICHEL DE MONTAIGNE

Talking about oneself can also be a means to conceal oneself.

FRIEDRICH NIETZSCHE

Nobody talks more passionately about his rights than he who,
in the depths of his soul, is doubtful about them.

FRIEDRICH NIETZSCHE

The greatest surprise of human evolution may be that
the highest form of selfishness is selflessness.

ROBERT ORNSTEIN

When men are ruled by fear,
they strive to prevent the very changes that will abate it.

ALAN PATON

Truth often suffers more by the heat of its defenders
than from the arguments of its opposers.

WILLIAM PENN

People wish to learn to swim and at the same time
to keep one foot on the ground.

MARCEL PROUST

We spend our time envying people who we wouldn't like to be.

JEAN ROSTAND

There is a law in human nature which
draws us to like what we passionately condemn.

GEORGE WILLIAM RUSSELL

People who are always thinking of the feelings of others
can be very destructive because
they are hiding so much from themselves.

MAY SARTON

Man is condemned to be free.

JEAN-PAUL SARTRE

We are all so much together, but we are dying of loneliness.

ALBERT SCHWEITZER

Night brings our troubles to the light, rather than banishes them.

SENECA (FIRST CENTURY A.D.)

There are no greater wretches in the world than
many of those whom people in general take to be happy.

SENECA (FIRST CENTURY A.D.)

No question is so difficult to answer
as that to which the answer is obvious.

GEORGE BERNARD SHAW

People get tired of everything,
and of nothing sooner than of what they most like.

GEORGE BERNARD SHAW

He who goes against the fashion is himself its slave.

LOGAN PEARSALL SMITH

Human beings cling to their delicious tyrannies
and to their exquisite nonsense, till death stares them in the face.

SYDNEY SMITH

The ultimate result of shielding men from the effects of folly
is to fill the world with fools.

HERBERT SPENCER

There is no fatigue so wearisome
as that which comes from lack of work.

CHARLES HADDON SPURGEON

We spend our time searching for security and hate it when we get it.

JOHN STEINBECK

There is a fellowship more quiet even than solitude,
and which, rightly understood, is solitude made perfect.

ROBERT LOUIS STEVENSON

It is a tragic paradox that the very qualities
that have led to man's extraordinary capacity for success
are also those most likely to destroy him.

ANTHONY STORR

Man is worse than an animal when he is an animal.

RABINDRANATH TAGORE

We succeed in enterprises which
demand the positive qualities we possess,
but we excel in those which can also make use of our defects.

ALEXIS DE TOCQUEVILLE

It is a paradoxical but profoundly true and important principle of life
that the most likely way to reach a goal
is to be aiming not at that goal itself
but at some more ambitious goal beyond it.

ARNOLD J. TOYNBEE

Success is the necessary misfortune of life,
but it is only to the very unfortunate that it comes early.

ANTHONY TROLLOPE

Often, the surest way to convey misinformation
is to tell the strict truth.

MARK TWAIN

There are two times in a man's life when he should not speculate:
when he can't afford it and when he can.

MARK TWAIN

The lazy are always wanting to do something.

MARQUIS DE VAUVENARGUES (LUC DE CLAPIERS)

Men will always be mad, and those who think
they can cure them are the maddest of all.

VOLTAIRE

At the moment you are most in awe
of all there is about life that you don't understand,
you are closer to understanding it all than at any other time.

JANE WAGNER

It is a curious thing that every creed promises a paradise which
will be absolutely uninhabitable for anyone of civilized taste.

EVELYN WAUGH

Imagination and fiction make up
more than three quarters of our real life.

SIMONE WEIL

It is very easy to forgive others their mistakes;
it takes more grit and gumption to forgive them
for having witnessed your own.

JESSAMYN WEST

There is nothing more likely to start disagreement
among people or countries than an agreement.

E. B. WHITE

It requires a very unusual mind
to undertake the analysis of the obvious.

ALFRED NORTH WHITEHEAD

It is because Humanity has never known where it was going
that it has been able to find its way.

OSCAR WILDE

Man can believe the impossible,
but can never believe the improbable.

OSCAR WILDE

No scientific theory achieves public acceptance
until it has been thoroughly discredited.

DOUGLAS YATES

People have one thing in common: they are all different.

ROBERT ZEND

chapter three

SEX, LOVE, & ROMANCE

In an eighteenth-century book titled *A Father's Legacy to His Daughters*, an Englishman writing under the pseudonym of Dr. Gregory offered fatherly advice to his daughters about life and love. In one memorable passage, he wrote:

> **A fine woman shows her charms to most advantage**
> **when she seems most to conceal them.**

Since concealed things are not supposed to be recognized at all, the concerned father's advice is a variation on the "less is more" theme. His point is that it's better to leave some things to the mind's eye. Or as he put it, "The finest bosom in nature is not so fine as imagination forms." Others have also written about this paradoxical aspect of feminine allure:

A woman is closest to being naked when she is well dressed.

COCO CHANEL

**What a man enjoys about a woman's clothes
are his fantasies of how she would look without them.**

BRENDAN BEHAN

**There is . . . no woman so naked as one
you can see to be naked under her clothes.**

MICHAEL FRAYN

For centuries, people have been writing about the convoluted, contradictory, and often very confusing patterns associated with matters of the heart. It's probably fair to say that no other arena of human activity has inspired more oxymoronic observations. Some of the best come from anonymous sources:

A man chases a woman until she catches him.

In the act of loving, you arm another person against you.

**A man is never so weak as when
a woman is telling him how strong he is.**

Another great one came from a 1948 issue of *The Ladies' Home Journal:*

It takes a lot of experience for a girl to kiss like a beginner.

When romantics rhapsodize about the glory of love, not everyone agrees. Realists and cynics, in particular, see the darker side of love, often pointing out its undisputed link with the baser aspects of human nature, including jealousy, control, hatred, and even violence. Yes, love may be the most ecstatic of human emotions, bringing heights of pleasure and even soothing some pretty savage beasts. But love can also be a source of deep pain. And in a fascinating twist, the pains of love are often a source of pleasure. Poets have said it well:

> **The sweetest joy, the wildest woe is love.**
>
> P. J. BAILEY

> **A mighty pain to love it is,**
> **And 'tis a pain that pain to miss.**
>
> ABRAHAM COWLEY

> **O what a heaven is love!**
> **O what a hell!**
>
> THOMAS MIDDLETON AND THOMAS DEKKER

> **Love begets love.**
> **This torment is my joy.**
>
> THEODORE ROETHKE

But perhaps the best description of the pleasurable pains of love comes from an eighteenth-century writer, George Colman the Younger:

> **What a recreation it is to be in love!**
> **It sets the heart aching so delicately,**
> **there's no taking a wink of sleep for the pleasure of the pain.**

In another paradox, love leads to both profound truth-telling and grand deceptions. While in the throes of love, people reveal things about themselves they would never disclose during more rational moments. And, conversely, when people are in hot romantic pursuit, they can perpetrate spectacular deceits. The artifices surrounding the courtship ritual are among the most interesting of all human behaviors. But even more fascinating than the behavior of the deceivers is the willingness of the deceived to go along with the charade. People hungry for love all too easily fall for words and actions that, at some level of their consciousness, they know to be patently untrue. They want to believe so badly that they accept the flimsiest evidence for what they want to hear. And, of course, they ignore the most solid evidence against it. Shakespeare described the situation beautifully in *Sonnet 138:*

> **When my love swears that she is made of truth,**
> **I do believe her, though I know she lies.**

Lord Byron advanced the same idea in *Don Juan:*

> **Now what I love in women is, they won't**
> **Or can't do otherwise than lie, but do it**
> **So well, the very truth seems false.**

Many writers have written about the loving lies of lying lovers. Here are a few of my personal favorites.

> **In love, assurances are practically an announcement of their opposite.**
>
> ELIAS CANETTI

> **Doubt the man who swears to his devotion.**
>
> LOUISE COLET

**In love-making, feigning lovers succeed
much better than the really devoted.**

NINON DE LENCLOS

Another one of love's fascinating convolutions has been a special
source of puzzlement to intelligent people who guide their lives
according to principles of reason—the tendency to be most strongly
attracted to people who are the worst for us. More than fifty years ago,
the psychologist Rudolf Dreikurs wrote:

**A great many people fall in love with or feel attracted to a person
who offers the least possibility of a harmonious union.**

In my work as a counselor and therapist, I've seen this kind of thing
occur many times over the years (and when I was single guy, I must
confess that I experienced it a time or two myself). Linda Barnes, in
her 1993 book *Snapshot*, has a character who is so familiar with this
pattern that she finally concludes:

**I have no-fail chemistry. A guy turns me on,
he's the wrong one for me.**

Of all the paradoxes of love, though, perhaps the most intriguing is
the inextricable historical connection that love has with hatred. When
the flames of love are burning, they burn intensely. But when love's
flames are extinguished, they don't necessarily turn cold. They often
transform into another intense emotion—hatred. It has been long recognized that the more intense the love, the greater the potential for
hatred when love eventually fades. Writing in the fifth century B.C.,
the Greek dramatist Euripides wrote:

**The worst, the least curable hatred
is that which has superseded deep love.**

The love-to-hate transformation has been described in many different ways by many different people throughout history:

Of all the objects of hatred, a woman once loved is the most hateful.

MAX BEERBOHM

**Heaven has no rage like love to hatred turned,
Nor hell a fury like a woman scorned.**

WILLIAM CONGREVE

The greatest hate springs from the greatest love.

THOMAS FULLER

Hatreds are the cinders of affection.

SIR WALTER RALEIGH

This morphing of love into hate has been such a predictable and pervasive aspect of human experience that the French aphorist La Rochefoucauld concluded:

**If we judge love by the majority of its results,
it rather resembles hatred than friendship.**

If love can lead to hatred, then it is only one additional step for hatred to lead to something even worse. We've already seen that hell has no fury like a woman scorned, but when male love turns into hatred it can get very ugly, as we see so frequently in news reports about domestic violence. Writing over a century ago, George Bernard Shaw described it this way:

> **When we want to read of the deeds that are done for love,**
> **whither do we turn?**
> **To the murder column; and there we are rarely disappointed.**

Before we get too depressed with all this talk of violence and murder, let me hasten to add that the hatred that often shows up in love is quite normal and predictable, and can even have a humorous component. The people we love can occasionally be so exasperating, frustrating, or just plain impossible that they stimulate feelings inside of us that can only be described by one word—hate. To form an oxymoron I don't recall seeing before, we could call it a *loving hatred*. This hybrid emotion shows up in the healthiest relationships and the strongest marriages, where love and hate achieve a kind of peaceful coexistence with each other. The Swedish dramatist August Strindberg described it eloquently:

> **I love her and she loves me, and we hate each other**
> **with a wild hatred born of love.**

But perhaps my favorite words on the subject come from that perceptive observer of domestic drama, Judith Viorst, who observed in a 1975 article in *Redbook* magazine:

> **Love is the same as like except you feel sexier. And more romantic.**
> **And also more annoyed when he talks with his mouth full.**
> **And you also resent it more when he interrupts you.**
> **And you also respect him less when he shows any weakness.**

And furthermore, when you ask him to pick you up at the airport
and he tells you he can't do it because he's busy,
it's only when you love him that you hate him.

So far we've only skimmed the surface when it comes to oxymoronic
observations about the world of sex, love, and romance. After reading
the rest of the quotes in the remainder of this chapter, you may never
see your love life—or the age-old struggle between the sexes—in the
same way again.

None are more struck with the charms of virtue in the fair sex than
those who, by their very admiration of it,
are carried to a desire of ruining it.

JOSEPH ADDISON

Love is the source of every virtue in you
and of every deed which deserves punishment.

DANTE ALIGHIERI

Love involves a peculiar unfathomable combination
of understanding and misunderstanding.

DIANE ARBUS

The most virtuous woman always has something within her
that is not quite chaste.

HONORÉ DE BALZAC

Men are so made that they can resist sound argument,
and yet yield to a glance.

HONORÉ DE BALZAC

Women, when they have made a sheep of a man,
always tell him that he is a lion with a will of iron.

HONORÉ DE BALZAC

The man who gets on best with women is the one
who knows best how to get on without them.

CHARLES BAUDELAIRE

Where love is concerned, too much is not even enough!

PIERRE DE BEAUMARCHAIS

To obtain a woman who loves you, you must treat her as if she didn't.

PIERRE DE BEAUMARCHAIS

The big difference between sex for money and sex for free
is that sex for money usually costs a lot less.

BRENDAN BEHAN

The physical union of the sexes
only intensifies man's sense of solitude.

NICOLAS BERDYAEV

In love, victory goes to the man who runs away.

NAPOLEON BONAPARTE

Such ever was love's way; to rise, it stoops.

ROBERT BROWNING

Girls have an unfair advantage over men:
if they can't get what they want by being smart,
they can get it by being dumb.

YUL BRYNNER

Of course, it's possible to love a human being—
if you don't know them too well.

CHARLES BUKOWSKI

The falling out of lovers is the renewing of love.

ROBERT BURTON

A woman smells best when she hath no perfume at all.

ROBERT BURTON

Nothing is potent against love save impotence.

SAMUEL BUTLER

Alas! the love of women! it is known
To be a lovely and a fearful thing.

LORD BYRON

Love and War are the same thing,
and stratagems and policy are as allowable in the one as in the other.

MIGUEL DE CERVANTES

There are two things I have always loved madly . . .
women and celibacy.

NICOLAS DE CHAMFORT

There are girls who manage to sell themselves
whom no one would take as gifts.

NICOLAS DE CHAMFORT

Great loves too must be endured.

COCO CHANEL

Next to the wound, what women make best is the bandage.

BARBEY D'AUREVILLY

What most men desire is a virgin who is a whore.

EDWARD DAHLBERG

We love what we should scorn if we were wiser.

MARIE DE FRANCE

A woman with eyes only for one person,
or with eyes always averted from him,
creates exactly the same impression.

JEAN DE LA BRUYÈRE

One seeks to make the loved one entirely happy,
or, if that cannot be, entirely wretched.

JEAN DE LA BRUYÈRE

Nothing is as varied as the pleasures of love,
although they are always the same.

NINON DE LENCLOS

Women are never stronger than when
they arm themselves with their weaknesses.

MARIE DU DEFFAND

Most women set out to try to change a man,
and when they have changed him they do not like him.

MARLENE DIETRICH

Woman inspires us to do great things,
and prevents us from achieving them.

ALEXANDRE DUMAS

You have to be very fond of men to love them.
Otherwise they're simply unbearable.

MARGUERITE DURAS

It is a common enough case, that of a man being suddenly captivated
by a woman nearly the opposite of his ideal.

GEORGE ELIOT

In love the paradox occurs that two beings become one
and yet remain two.

ERICH FROMM

To make a young couple love each other,
it is only necessary to oppose and separate them.

JOHANN WOLFGANG VON GOETHE

The tragedy is not that love doesn't last.
The tragedy is the love that lasts.

SHIRLEY HAZZARD

If two people love each other there can be no happy end to it.

ERNEST HEMINGWAY

The love we give away is the only love we keep.

ELBERT HUBBARD

A woman is more responsive to a man's forgetfulness
than to his attentions.

JULES JANIN

The only thing worse than a man you can't control is a man you can.

MARGO KAUFMAN

The beauty of a strong, lasting commitment
is often best understood by a man incapable of it.

MURRAY KEMPTON

Personally I think if a woman hasn't met the right man
by the time she's twenty-four, she may be lucky.

DEBORAH KERR

Perfect love means to love the one
through whom one became unhappy.

SØREN KIERKEGAARD

The more we love a mistress, the nearer we are to hating her.

LA ROCHEFOUCAULD

Women in love forgive large indiscretions
more easily than small infidelities.

LA ROCHEFOUCAULD

Sex is the one thing you cannot really swindle;
and it is the center of the worst swindling of all, emotional swindling.

D. H. LAWRENCE

Their bodies were so close together that
there was no room for real affection.

STANISLAW LEC

Paradoxically, we cannot navigate clearly within a relationship
unless we can live without it.

HARRIET G. LERNER

Only love can be divided endlessly and still not diminish.

ANNE MORROW LINDBERGH

Women are perfectly well aware
that the more they seem to obey the more they rule.

JULES MICHELET

Tranquility in love is a disagreeable calm.

MOLIÈRE

Sex touches the heavens only when it simultaneously
touches the gutter and the mud.

GEORGE JEAN NATHAN

We think about sex obsessively except during the act,
when our minds tend to wander.

HOWARD NEMEROV

It may be true that a touch of indifference is the safest foundation
on which to build a lasting and delicate friendship.

W. ROBERTSON NICOLL

Love commingled with hate is more powerful than love. Or hate.

JOYCE CAROL OATES

The longest absence is less perilous to love
than the terrible trials of incessant proximity.

OUIDA (MARIE LOUISE DE LA RAMÉE)

Love is a kind of warfare.

OVID (FIRST CENTURY A.D.)

Women often wish to give unwillingly what they really like to give.

OVID (FIRST CENTURY A.D.)

Scratch a lover and find a foe.

DOROTHY PARKER

To be able to say how much you love is to love but little.

PETRARCH (FRANCESCO PETRARCA)

In a separation, it is the one who is not really in love
who says the most tender things.

MARCEL PROUST

Oh, I have loved him too much to feel no hate for him.

JEAN RACINE

This is the miracle that happens every time to those who really love:
the more they give, the more they possess.

RAINER MARIA RILKE

Failing to be there when a man wants her is a woman's greatest sin,
except to be there when he doesn't want her.

HELEN ROWLAND

Human nature is so constructed that it gives affection most readily
to those who seem least to demand it.

BERTRAND RUSSELL

I like men to behave like men—strong and childish.

FRANÇOISE SAGAN

All the sweetness of love is steeped
In bitter gall and deadly venom.

MAURICE SCÈVE

I made no advances to her, but she accepted them.

LOUIS SCUTENAIRE

You can end love more easily than you can moderate it.

SENECA THE ELDER (FIRST CENTURY A.D.)

Love gets people into difficulties, not out of them.

GEORGE BERNARD SHAW

One of the advantages of living alone
is that you don't have to wake up in the arms of a loved one.

ANNA MARION SMITH

Once made equal to a man, woman becomes his superior.

SOCRATES (FIFTH CENTURY B.C.)

The penalty for getting the woman you want
is that you must keep her.

LIONEL STRACHEY

I hated her now with a hatred more fatal than indifference
because it was the other side of love.

AUGUST STRINDBERG

Antipathy, dissimilarity of views, hate, contempt,
can accompany true love.

AUGUST STRINDBERG

To love deeply in one direction makes us more loving in all others.

ANNE SWETCHINE

Only when a women is openly bad is she really good.

PUBLILIUS SYRUS (FIRST CENTURY B.C.)

No one worth possessing can be quite possessed.

SARA TEASDALE

Lovers' quarrels are the renewal of love.

TERENCE (SECOND CENTURY B.C.)

Those whom we can love, we can hate; to others we are indifferent.

HENRY DAVID THOREAU

The best thing about being attracted to unavailable men
is that they're always available.

MEG TILLEY

If I had had a pistol I would have shot him—
either that or fallen at his feet.
There is no middle way when one loves.

LADY LAURA TROUBRIDGE

A bad woman always has something she regards as a curse—
a real bit of goodness hidden away somewhere.

LADY LAURA TROUBRIDGE

Sex is like money; only too much is enough.

JOHN UPDIKE

God created man and, finding him not sufficiently alone,
gave him a companion to make him feel his solitude more keenly.

PAUL VALÉRY

An intelligent woman is a woman with whom
we can be as stupid as we like.

PAUL VALÉRY

We love people, and we say that
we were going to do more for them than friendship,
but it makes such fools of us that we do far less,
indeed sometimes what we do
could be mistaken for the work of hatred.

REBECCA WEST

The real paradox is that the men who make, materially,
the biggest sacrifices for their women
should do the least for them ideally and romantically.

EDITH WHARTON

It is difficult not to be unjust to what one loves.

OSCAR WILDE

A man can be happy with any woman as long as he does not love her.

OSCAR WILDE

The two sexes mutually corrupt and improve each other.

MARY WOLLSTONECRAFT

chapter four

MARRIAGE, HOME, & FAMILY LIFE

In January of 1814, Lord Byron married Anne Isabella Milbanke. Shortly before the marriage, he wrote in a letter to a friend:

> **I am about to be married—and am of course
> in all the misery of a man in pursuit of happiness.**

The best lines from great writers and poets often come not from their published works, but from their private correspondence. Such is the case here, as Byron so cleverly describes the ambivalence he felt about his upcoming marriage. It is appropriate that he used oxymoronic phrasing to describe his feelings, for the institution of marriage is filled with numerous twists and turns, many of which are unexpected and perplexing. It starts when different people—indeed, people who often seem to come from different planets—try to carve out a life together. Then, as if the dynamics of married life were not complex enough, children arrive, further complicating an already challenging situation. Happily, observers of the domestic scene have been around for centuries, and they have recorded the many paradoxical aspects of marriage, home, and family life.

People decide to marry for many reasons, but one of the most common motives throughout history is to escape the pain of being single. After marrying, though, many don't achieve the companionship they hoped for. Instead, they discover in their marriages an even more painful feeling of solitude. You see, the worst kind of loneliness comes to people who are, technically, not alone. The Russian writer Anton Chekhov, who was aware of this problem, even went so far as to advise:

If you are afraid of loneliness, don't marry.

Others have also written about this predictable aspect of married life:

Marriage is lonelier than solitude.

ADRIENNE RICH

The surest way to be alone is to get married.

GLORIA STEINEM

**Marriage is the only thing that
affords a woman the pleasure of company
and the perfect sensation of solitude at the same time.**

HELEN ROWLAND

Sadly, many couples discover in their marriages something far worse than an unexpected solitude. These are people who, as the old saying goes, have jumped out of the frying pan and into the fire. As a marriage counselor for more than twenty-five years, I saw it happen many times—people who were miserable when they were single became even more miserable after they married. It's a great human irony, best described by the French essayist Montaigne, when he wrote about marriage:

> **It may be compared to a cage,**
> **the birds without try desperately to get in,**
> **and those within try desperately to get out.**

What can we conclude when single people yearn to be married and married people long to be single? After centuries of human experience, is the better choice to remain single or to marry? A number of wry observers of the human scene have come up with surprisingly similar—and of course, oxymoronic—answers:

> **One was never married, and that's his hell;**
> **Another is, and that's his plague.**
>
> ROBERT BURTON

> **Matrimony and bachelorhood are both of them**
> **at once equally wise and equally foolish.**
>
> SAMUEL BUTLER

> **It doesn't matter whether you decide to marry or stay single;**
> **either way you'll be sorry.**
>
> SOCRATES

The American writer and humorist Edgar Watson Howe extended the same logic to another major life decision—to have children or not:

**Families with babies and families without babies
are sorry for each other.**

While marriage sometimes turns out to be a nightmare, it's important to note that it can also turn out to be blissful. So, in another paradox, marriage can be one of the best and one of the worst things to happen to people. The eighteenth-century English writer Thomas Fuller was writing from a male perspective, but his observation about this fact of life could be easily modified to apply to women:

A man's best fortune, or his worst, is his wife.

At some point, most marriages produce children, transforming a married couple into a completely new entity—a family. This can also lead to problems, as couples quite naturally begin to focus their attention on the new arrival and take their eyes off each other. Marriage counselors have long joked that children can be hazardous to a marriage. While there is some truth to that remark, the reality is that the responsibilities of parenthood usually help people become more mature. In another hybrid example of chiasmus and oxymoronica, the American writer Peter De Vries described it this way:

**The value of marriage is not
that adults produce children,
but that children produce adults.**

When people embark on the adventure of parenthood, most plan to raise their children in a supportive and loving environment. It's a wonderful ideal, of course, but not without some danger, especially when parents make the fairly common mistake of loving their children too much. As shown elsewhere in these pages, one of the oldest oxymoronic themes in history is that too much of a good thing is bad.

This principle applies as well in parenting as in any other sector of human life. It also has some predictable consequences. One was described by the English writer Sir Henry Taylor:

A spoiled child never loves his mother.

Parents who spoil their children tend to be insecure. By lavishing their children and failing to discipline or set limits, they attempt to win the love and approval of their children. As Taylor makes clear, however, the strategy doesn't work. To make matters worse, spoiling children has the additional disadvantage of producing insufferable adults. This aspect of family life has been well known for centuries. In his 1625 play *Women Beware Women*, the English playwright Thomas Middleton wrote:

> **It is**
> **The fortune commonly of knavish children**
> **To have the loving'st mothers.**

More recently, the popular mystery writer P. D. James provided cautionary words about what can happen when children are treated a little too well:

> **If from infancy you treat children as gods**
> **they are liable in adulthood to act as devils.**

George Bernard Shaw wrote about one other negative consequence that can result from families who love too much, and he did so quite cleverly:

> **All my life, affection has been showered upon me,**
> **and every forward step I have made has been taken in spite of it.**

Shaw provides an intriguing suggestion about why too much family affection can be a bad thing—if children get it when they know it's undeserved, it may retard their growth. The English writer W. Somerset Maugham echoed Shaw's sentiment when he wrote:

> **Few misfortunes can befall a boy which bring worse consequences than to have a really affectionate mother.**

How is it that family affection can have such an untoward effect? The eighteenth-century German physicist and philosopher G. C. Lichtenberg offered an explanation:

> **To receive applause for works which do not demand all our powers hinders our advance towards a perfecting of our spirit.
> It usually means that thereafter we stand still.**

Another parenting technique that backfires is permissiveness. To the extent that permissive parents have a purpose, it is to help children grow up. Many justify their behavior by saying that they're simply trying to treat their children like adults. But permissiveness rarely achieves the goal of helping children grow up, and often, inadvertently, produces just the opposite—emotionally immature adults. The psychologist Thomas Szasz described it well:

> **Permissiveness is the principle of treating children as if they were adults;
> and the tactic of making sure they never reach that stage.**

When kids become problems for their parents, it's not always a horror story, and sometimes even has humorous or endearing aspects. Mark Twain said it best in one of his most popular observations:

> **My mother had a great deal of trouble with me, but I think she enjoyed it.**

In the rest of this chapter, let's take a look at more oxymoronic observations about marriage, home, and family life. It's a pretty wide-ranging collection of quotes, but all of them have been selected to stimulate your thinking about the family you grew up in, the families all around you, and the family you are part of today.

> I read about divorce, and I can't see
> why two people can't get along together in harmony,
> and I see two people and I can't see
> how either of them can live with each other.
>
> FRANKLIN P. ADAMS

> It is a great happiness to see our children rising round us,
> but from that good fortune spring the bitterest woes of man.
>
> AESCHYLUS (FIFTH CENTURY B.C.)

> Of course a platonic relationship is possible—
> but only between husband and wife.
>
> ANONYMOUS, FROM *LADIES' HOME JOURNAL*

> It's never too late to have a happy childhood.
>
> ANONYMOUS

> After winning an argument with his wife,
> the wisest thing a man can do is apologize.
>
> ANONYMOUS

> Marriage always demands the greatest understanding of
> the art of insincerity possible between two human beings.
>
> VICKI BAUM

> Bride, *n.* A woman with a fine prospect of happiness behind her.
>
> AMBROSE BIERCE

A mother starts out as the most important person in her child's world,
and if she's successful in her work,
she will eventually become the stupidest.

MARY KAY BLAKELY

The average child is an almost non-existent myth.
To be normal one must be peculiar in some way or another.

HEYWOOD BROUN

Parents are the last people on earth who ought to have children.

SAMUEL BUTLER

People marry for a variety of reasons, and with varying results;
but to marry for love is to invite inevitable tragedy.

JAMES BRANCH CABELL

Personal hatred and family affection are not incompatible;
they often flourish and grow strong together.

WILLA CATHER

Bachelors' wives and old maids' children are always perfect.

NICOLAS CHAMFORT

Something you consider bad may bring out your child's talents;
something you consider good may stifle them.

FRANÇOIS RENÉ DE CHATEAUBRIAND

Pregnancy is difficult for women but it is even more difficult for men.

SUSAN CHEEVER

I cannot bear the crying of children,
but when my child cries, I don't hear.

ANTON CHEKHOV

The only people who seem to have nothing to do
with the education of the children are the parents.

G. K. CHESTERTON

Playing as children means playing
is the most serious thing in the world.

G. K. CHESTERTON

Nobody knows how to manage a wife but a bachelor.

GEORGE COLMAN THE ELDER

Two important things to teach a child: to do and to do without.

MARCELENE COX

The young always have the same problem—
how to rebel and conform at the same time.
They have now solved this by defying their parents
and copying one another.

QUENTIN CRISP

Harold and I didn't get along badly for married people,
but the problem was I didn't misunderstand him.
No marriage can be completely successful
without a reasonable amount of misunderstanding.

LILLIAN DAY

"Our union has been blest with issues," I said.

PETER DE VRIES

When I can no longer bear to think of the victims of broken homes,
I begin to think of the victims of intact ones.

PETER DE VRIES

I have always thought that every woman should marry, and no man.

BENJAMIN DISRAELI

An obedient wife commands her husband.

BENJAMIN DISRAELI

Nobody can misunderstand a boy like his own mother.

NORMAN DOUGLAS

The complaints which anyone voices against his mate indicate
exactly the qualities which stimulated attraction before marriage.

RUDOLF DREIKURS

The only good husbands stay bachelors;
they're too considerate to get married.

FINLEY PETER DUNNE

Parents forgive their children least readily
for the faults they themselves instilled in them.

MARIE VON EBNER-ESCHENBACH

The finest people marry the two sexes in their own person.

RALPH WALDO EMERSON

Let your children go if you want to keep them.

MALCOLM FORBES

There is no power greater than the power of passive dependency.

MARILYN FRENCH

A girl must marry for love, and keep on marrying until she finds it.

ZSA ZSA GABOR

We want our children to fit in and to stand out.
We rarely address the conflict between these goals.

ELLEN GOODMAN

When a man steals your wife, there is
no better revenge than to let him keep her.

SACHA GUITRY

No stranger can get a great many notes of torture out of a human soul;
it takes one that knows it well—
parent, child, brother, sister, intimate.

OLIVER WENDELL HOLMES SR.

The object of teaching a child is to enable him
to get along without his teacher.

ELBERT HUBBARD

The proper time to influence the character of a child
is about a hundred years before he is born.

W. R. INGE

Marriage is a mistake every man should make.

GEORGE JESSEL

When family relations are no longer harmonious,
we have filial children and devoted parents.

R. D. LAING

I am determined my children shall be brought up
in their father's religion, if they can find out what it is.

CHARLES LAMB

The unhappiness of a wife with a good husband
is much more devastating than
the unhappiness of a wife with a bad husband.

D. H. LAWRENCE

I suspect that in every good marriage
there are times when love seems to be over.

MADELEINE L'ENGLE

We all of us wanted babies—but did we want children?

EDA J. LESHAN

If you are a parent it helps if you are a grown-up.

EDA J. LESHAN

Always remember . . . it's matrimonial suicide
to be jealous when you have a really good reason.

CLARE BOOTHE LUCE

Adultery is a meanness and a stealing,
a taking away from someone what should be theirs, a great selfishness,
and surrounded and guarded by lies lest it be found out.
And out of the meanness and selfishness and lying flow
love and joy and peace beyond anything that can be imagined.

DAME ROSE MACAULAY

I'd always rather be with people who loved me too little
rather than with people who loved me too much.

KATHERINE MANSFIELD

The wife should be inferior to the husband.
That is the only way to insure equality between the two.

MARTIAL (FIRST CENTURY A.D.)

You're obstinate, pliant, merry, morose, all at once.
For me there's no living with you, or without you.

MARTIAL (FIRST CENTURY A.D.)

When a man brings his wife flowers for no reason—
there's a reason.

MOLLY MCGEE

The fault no child ever loses is the one he was most punished for.

MIGNON MCLAUGHLIN

Most of us become parents long before
we have stopped being children.

MIGNON MCLAUGHLIN

The way to hold a husband is to keep him a little jealous;
the way to lose him is to keep him a little more jealous.

H. L. MENCKEN

Each one of an affectionate couple may be willing . . .
to die for the other, yet unwilling
to utter the agreeable word at the right moment.

GEORGE MEREDITH

I love children, especially when they cry,
for then someone takes them away.

NANCY MITFORD

The principle contributor to loneliness in this country is television.
What happens is that the family "gets together" alone.

ASHLEY MONTAGU

If married couples did not live together,
happy marriages would be more frequent.

FRIEDRICH NIETZSCHE

When one has not had a good father, one must create one.

FRIEDRICH NIETZSCHE

Everybody knows how to raise children,
except the people who have them.

P. J. O'ROURKE

Babies are always more trouble than you thought—
and more wonderful.

CHARLES OSGOOD

A good marriage is that in which
each appoints the other guardian of his solitude.

RAINER MARIA RILKE

There's no one more depressed than a happily married man.

MICKEY ROONEY

A good father is a little bit of a mother.

LEE SALK

Fond as we are of loved ones, there comes at times
during their absence an unexplained peace.

ANNE SHAW

Housework, if it's done right, can kill you.

JOHN SKOW

The American girl makes a servant of her husband
and then finds him contemptible for being a servant.

JOHN STEINBECK

Some of us are becoming the men we wanted to marry.

GLORIA STEINEM

If a man's character is to be abused,
there's nobody like a relative to do the business.

WILLIAM MAKEPEACE THACKERAY

How do I hate those words "an excellent marriage."
In them is contained more of wicked worldliness
than any other words one ever hears spoken.

ANTHONY TROLLOPE

A baby is an inestimable blessing and bother.

MARK TWAIN

Never have children, only grandchildren.

GORE VIDAL

A normal adolescent isn't a normal adolescent if he acts normal.

JUDITH VIORST

One can always recognize women who trust their husbands;
they look so thoroughly unhappy.

OSCAR WILDE

There is nothing in the world like the devotion of a married woman.
It's a thing no married man knows anything about.

OSCAR WILDE

The child is father of the man.

WILLIAM WORDSWORTH

chapter five

ANCIENT OXYMORONICA

R alph Waldo Emerson once observed:

All my best thoughts were stolen by the ancients.

Stolen by the ancients? How can people from centuries ago steal ideas from modern thinkers? Of course, they can't. But this is Emerson's way of describing a fairly common and somewhat bittersweet experience. We come up with what seems like a genuinely original thought, often taking some pride in doing so. But then we discover that someone else beat us to the punch, authoring the same sentiment years, even centuries, before. It's happened to me a number of times, and I'll bet it has happened to you as well. It's a little deflating at first, but ultimately pretty satisfying to discover that we have briefly been on the same wavelength with some of the world's finest thinkers.

In a fitting irony, an ancient thinker, the Roman grammarian

Aelius Donatus, purloined Emerson's observation. Donatus occupies a footnote in history as the teacher of St. Jerome. The student once quoted his teacher as complaining:

Confound those who have made our comments before us.

As it turns out, the ancients have been guilty of far more intellectual theft than even Emerson suspected. And nowhere is this more true than in the realm of oxymoronica, where many modern-sounding ideas were first offered in the earliest days of civilization.

Today, for example, it has become a cliché for people to say that getting what we want is not necessarily the best thing for us. Oscar Wilde put it this way:

**In this world there are only two tragedies.
One is not getting what one wants and the other is getting it.**

In a very similar vein, George Bernard Shaw wrote:

**There are two tragedies in life.
One is to lose your heart's desire. The other is to gain it.**

In my research, I've discovered that these two observations are part of what might be called a grand oxymoronic theme. I now have several dozen quotes—almost all from modern thinkers—that make the point that getting what we want is bad for us. Here are just a few examples:

Be careful what you set your heart upon—for it will surely be yours.

JAMES BALDWIN

**How many of our daydreams would darken into nightmares,
were there any danger of their coming true.**

LOGAN PEARSALL SMITH

More tears are shed over answered prayers than unanswered ones.
MOTHER TERESA

A contemporary idea? Hardly. In a perfect example of modern thoughts being appropriated by the ancients, Aesop in his famous fable "The Old Man and Death" wrote in the sixth century B.C.:

We would often be sorry if our wishes were gratified.

A century after Aesop, the Greek philosopher Heraclitus echoed the sentiment:

It would not be better for mankind if they were given their desires.

Another popular oxymoronic theme has to do with the search for happiness. Many modern writers have expressed the same idea in slightly different ways:

**Some of us might find happiness if we would
quit struggling so desperately for it.**
WILLIAM FEATHER

The search for happiness is one of the chief sources of unhappiness.
ERIC HOFFER

**Men can only be happy when they
do not assume that the object of life is happiness.**
GEORGE ORWELL

Happiness is not best achieved by those who seek it directly.
BERTRAND RUSSELL

**The greatest happiness you can have is knowing that you
do not necessarily require happiness.**

WILLIAM SAROYAN

In another illustration of a modern idea being pilfered by the ancients, the Chinese sage Chuang-Tzu, writing in the fourth century B.C., appears to be the first person in history to note that seeking happiness is the worst way to find it:

Perfect happiness is the absence of striving for happiness.

Another popular oxymoronic theme has to do with the "sounds of silence." Literally, silence is the absence of sound. But when poets talk of "a thundering silence" or people say things like "His silence spoke volumes," they're communicating the notion that silence can often say much more than words. Many modern thinkers have expressed this idea, but once again we discover that the sentiment is ancient. Writing in the first century B.C., the Roman orator and statesman Cicero said:

Their very silence is a loud cry.

And four centuries before Cicero, the Greek lyric poet known as Pindar wrote:

Often silence is the wisest thing for a man to heed.

I mentioned earlier that "less is more" is one of the best-known examples of oxymoronica. First authored by Robert Browning in his 1855 poem "Andrea del Sarto," the sentiment turns out to be not so modern after all. In the eighth century B.C., the Greek poet Hesiod wrote what may be the earliest articulation of the idea:

The half is greater than the whole.

And in the first century B.C., the Roman philosopher and statesman Seneca applied the concept to the psychological domain, writing in *Agamemnon:*

Who shrinks from knowledge of his calamities aggravates his fear;
troubles half seen do torture.

No discussion of ancient oxymoronica would be complete without briefly mentioning the great religious texts. Indeed, an entire volume could be devoted to the use of paradox in sacred writing. Let me present only a few examples here, including these from the Talmud:

Who wins through evil loses.

When you add to the truth, you subtract from it.

Some men study so much, they don't have time to know.

And these from the Bible:

It is possible to give away and become richer.

PROVERBS 11:24

My strength is made perfect in weakness.

2 CORINTHIANS 12:9

Woe unto you, when all men shall speak well of you.

LUKE 6:26

Lead me to a rock that is too high.

PSALMS 61:2

This last passage is a wonderful articulation of the idea of setting noble goals. These days, counselors, coaches, and consultants often speak of reaching for the stars or setting "stretch" goals. Robert Browning recommended something similar when he wrote, "Ah, a man's reach should exceed his grasp/Or what's a heaven for?" But, as we see with this Old Testament passage, aspiring toward lofty goals is an ancient idea.

In the remainder of this chapter, I present more examples of ancient oxymoronica. As you progress through the quotes, notice how many ancient insights are reflected in some of your favorite modern-day observations.

> **It is a profitable thing, if one is wise, to seem foolish.**
>
> AESCHYLUS, IN *PROMETHEUS BOUND*
> (FIFTH CENTURY B.C.)

> **We often give our enemies the means for our own destruction.**
>
> AESOP, IN "THE EAGLE AND THE ARROW"
> (SIXTH CENTURY B.C.)

> **We often despise what is most useful to us.**
>
> AESOP, IN "THE HART AND THE HUNTER"

> **Please all, and you will please none.**
>
> AESOP, IN "THE MAN, THE BOY, AND THE DONKEY"

> **Play so that you may be serious.**
>
> ANACHARSIS, QUOTED BY HERODOTUS
> (SIXTH CENTURY B.C.)

> **Even if you persuade me, you won't persuade me.**
>
> ARISTOPHANES, IN *PLUTUS*
> (FOURTH CENTURY B.C.)

Quite often good things have hurtful consequences.
There are instances of men who have been
ruined by their money or killed by their courage.

ARISTOTLE, IN *NICHOMACHEAN ETHICS*
(FOURTH CENTURY B.C.)

Man wishes to be happy even when
he so lives as to make happiness impossible.

SAINT AUGUSTINE, IN *THE CITY OF GOD*
(FOURTH CENTURY A.D.)

Man is often vainglorious about his contempt of glory.

SAINT AUGUSTINE, IN *CONFESSIONS*

God is best known in not knowing Him.

SAINT AUGUSTINE, IN *DE ORDINE*

Submit to the fate of your own free will.

MARCUS AURELIUS, IN *MEDITATIONS*
(SECOND CENTURY A.D.)

I often marvel that while each man
loves himself more than anyone else,
he sets less value on his own estimate than on the opinions of others.

MARCUS AURELIUS, IN *MEDITATIONS*

Even in a palace life may be lived well.

MARCUS AURELIUS, IN *MEDITATIONS*
(SECOND CENTURY A.D.)

Hasten slowly. (in Latin, *Festina lente*)

AUGUSTUS CAESAR, QUOTED BY SUETONIUS
(FIRST CENTURY A.D.)

As a rule, what is out of sight
disturbs men's minds more seriously than what they see.

JULIUS CAESAR, IN *GALLIC WARS*

(FIRST CENTURY A.D.)

Suffer women once to arrive at an equality with you,
and they will from that moment become your superiors.

CATO THE CENSOR

(THIRD CENTURY B.C.)

All men know the utility of useful things;
but they do not know the utility of futility.

CHUANG-TZU, IN *THIS HUMAN WORLD*

(FOURTH CENTURY B.C.)

A man who knows he is a fool is not a great fool.

CHUANG-TZU, IN *WRITINGS*

There is something pleasurable in
calm remembrance of a past sorrow.

CICERO, IN *AD FAMILIARES*

(FIRST CENTURY B.C.)

Extreme justice is extreme injustice.

CICERO, IN *DE OFFICIIS*

Too much liberty leads both men and nations to slavery.

CICERO, IN *DE REPUBLICA*

Real knowledge is to know the extent of one's own ignorance.

CONFUCIUS, IN *ANALECTS*

(SIXTH CENTURY B.C.)

Study the past, if you would divine the future.

CONFUCIUS, IN *ANALECTS*

In a philosophical dispute, he gains most
who is defeated, since he learns most.

EPICURUS, IN *THE SAYING OF EPICURUS*
(FOURTH CENTURY B.C.)

Poverty, when measured by the natural purpose of life, is great wealth,
but unlimited wealth is great poverty.

EPICURUS, IN *THE SAYINGS OF EPICURUS*

Religion is a disease, but it is a noble disease.

HERACLITUS, IN *FRAGMENTS*
(FIFTH CENTURY B.C.)

Nothing is permanent but change.

HERACLITUS, IN *FRAGMENTS*

Too much rest itself becomes a pain.

HOMER, IN *THE ODYSSEY*
(EIGHTH CENTURY B.C.)

Nature is harmony in discord.

HORACE, IN *EPISTULAE*
(FIRST CENTURY B.C.)

To save a man's life against his will is the same as killing him.

HORACE, IN *ARS POETICA*

Poverty-stricken in the midst of great riches.

HORACE, IN *ODES*

When we try to avoid one fault we are led to the opposite,
unless we are very careful.

HORACE, IN *ARS POETICA*

A jest often decides matters of importance
more effectually and happily than seriousness.

HORACE

We all live in a state of ambitious poverty.

JUVENAL, IN *SATIRES*
(FIRST CENTURY A.D.)

We are now suffering the evils of a long peace.
Luxury, more deadly than war, broods over the city,
and avenges a conquered world.

JUVENAL, IN *SATIRES*

Honesty is praised and starves.

JUVENAL, IN *SATIRES*

The further one pursues knowledge, the less one knows.

LAO-TZU, IN *THE WAY OF LAO-TZU*
(SIXTH CENTURY B.C.)

Softness triumphs over hardness, feebleness over strength.
What is malleable is always superior to that which is immovable.
This is the principle of controlling things by going along with them,
of mastery through adaptation.

LAO-TZU, IN *THE WAY OF LAO-TZU*

The sage never strives for the great,
and thereby the great is achieved.

LAO-TZU, IN *THE WAY OF LAO-TZU*

One may know the world without going out of doors.
One may see the Way of Heaven
without looking through the windows.

LAO-TZU, IN *THE WAY OF LAO-TZU*

He has true glory that despises it.

LIVY, IN *THE HISTORY OF ROME*
(FIRST CENTURY A.D.)

In great attempts, it is glorious even to fail.

LONGINUS, IN *ON THE SUBLIME*
(FIRST CENTURY A.D.)

The only wealth which you will keep forever
is the wealth which you have given away.

MARTIAL, IN *EPIGRAMS*
(FIRST CENTURY A.D.)

A man who lives everywhere lives nowhere.

MARTIAL, IN *EPIGRAMS*

The path of duty lies in what is near,
and man seeks for it in what is remote.

MENCIUS, IN *WORKS*
(FOURTH CENTURY B.C.)

She is only constant in her inconstancy.

OVID, IN *TRISTIA*
(FIRST CENTURY B.C.)

Attention to health is the greatest hindrance to life.

PLATO, IN *DIALOGUES*
(FOURTH CENTURY B.C.)

There is simple ignorance, which is the source of lighter offenses,
and double ignorance, which is accompanied by a conceit of wisdom.

PLATO, IN *DIALOGUES*

A woman smells good when she smells of nothing.

PLAUTUS, IN *MOSTELLARIA*
(SECOND CENTURY B.C.)

To blow and swallow at the same moment is not easy.

PLAUTUS, IN *MOSTELLARIA*

They are twice as much friends as they were before quarreling.

PLAUTUS, IN *MOSTELLARIA*

The only certainty is that nothing is certain.

PLINY THE YOUNGER, IN *LETTERS*
(FIRST CENTURY A.D.)

His only fault is that he has no fault.

PLINY THE YOUNGER, IN *LETTERS*

Medicine, to produce health, has to examine disease;
and music, to create harmony, must investigate discord.

PLUTARCH, IN *LIVES*
(FIRST CENTURY A.D.)

Nothing is cheap which is superfluous,
for what one does not need, is dear at a penny.

PLUTARCH, IN *LIVES*

Agamemnon: What can a victor fear?
Cassandra: What he doth not fear.

SENECA, IN *AGAMEMNON*
(FIRST CENTURY A.D.)

It is for the superfluous we sweat.

SENECA, IN *LETTERS TO LUCILIUS*

He that is everywhere is nowhere.

SENECA, IN *LETTERS TO LUCILIUS*

I was shipwrecked before I got aboard.

SENECA, IN *LETTERS TO LUCILIUS*

The worst evil of all is to leave the ranks of the living before one dies.

SENECA, IN *MORAL ESSAYS*

You win the victory when you yield to friends.

SOPHOCLES, IN *AJAX*
(FIRST CENTURY B.C.)

To do two things at once is to do neither.

PUBLILIUS SYRUS, IN *MORAL SAYINGS*
(FIRST CENTURY B.C.)

Better to be ignorant of a matter than to half know it.

PUBLILIUS SYRUS, IN *MORAL SAYINGS*

He who yields a prudent obedience exercises a partial control.

PUBLILIUS SYRUS, IN *MORAL SAYINGS*

Agreement is made more precious by disagreement.

PUBLILIUS SYRUS, IN *MORAL SAYINGS*

It is a sin peculiar to man to hate his victim.

TACITUS, IN *AGRICOLA*
(SECOND CENTURY A.D.)

That worst class of enemies—the men who praise.

TACITUS, IN *AGRICOLA*

More faults are often committed while we are trying to oblige
than while we are giving offense.

TACITUS, IN *ANNALS*

To show resentment at a reproach
is to acknowledge that one may have deserved it.

TACITUS, IN *ANNALS*

He destroys his health by laboring to preserve it.

VIRGIL, IN *ECLOGUES*
(FIRST CENTURY B.C.)

chapter six

POLITICAL OXYMORONICA

The great French writer and critic Paul Valéry once wrote:

**Politics is the art of preventing people
from taking part in affairs which properly concern them.**

As with many wry comments, there's a great deal of truth embedded in Valéry's words. Politicians throughout history—once in positions of power—have often been inclined to keep citizens away from the affairs of state. This is especially true when citizens are disgruntled and critical of the way things are being done.

Politicians—and before them all of history's rulers—have long wrestled with the problem of what to do with opponents and dissenters. The natural tendency has been to silence critics by various means, ranging from censorship to assassination. But such methods always prove ineffective in the long run. As Voltaire once wrote:

**It is characteristic of the most stringent censorships
that they give credibility to the opinions they attack.**

This is a great counterintuitive truth, since the goal of censorship is to silence critics, not give them credibility. Voltaire went on to offer some important oxymoronic advice to government officials:

**If you are desirous to prevent the overrunning of a state
by any sect, show it toleration.**

Some countries, notably the great democracies of the West, have recognized the problems associated with silencing the opposition and have adopted the paradoxical remedy of giving opponents a platform. The reasoning was that giving critics a voice would actually make for a better government. The most famous statement of this idea appeared in Benjamin Disraeli's 1844 book *Coningsby*:

No government can be long secure without formidable opposition.

How can a government be secure when the opposition is formidable? The answer lies in a paradoxical truth about governance. The weakest governments silence their opposition and, in so doing, have no adversaries to keep them on their toes. The strongest governments give their opposition a voice, and—in theory at least—are willing to make changes necessary to govern more effectively. In 1790, the English statesman and political thinker Edmund Burke captured this set of ideas with a neat oxymoronic observation:

**A state without some means of change
is without the means of its conservation.**

The notion that governments must change to endure is at the heart of all great democracies. The thought has been expressed succinctly:

Reform, that you may preserve.

THOMAS BABINGTON MACAULAY

We must reform if we would conserve.

FRANKLIN DELANO ROOSEVELT

In his 1954 book *Freedom, Loyalty, and Dissent*, the American historian Henry Steele Commager said it this way:

If our democracy is to flourish, it must have criticism;
if our government is to function, it must have dissent.

At no time in the twentieth century did we see dissent expressed so vigorously in America as during the Vietnam War. During those tumultuous times, Senator J. William Fulbright of Arkansas became one of the most vocal critics of American policy. A few years prior, in a 1966 speech to the American Newspaper Publishers Association, he gave a clue as to how he felt about loyal dissent:

The citizen who criticizes his country is paying it an implied tribute.

If criticizing one's country is a form of tribute, then the next step would be to suggest that breaking the country's laws can be—paradoxically— a way of respecting them. Martin Luther King Jr. expressed this very idea when he said:

An individual who breaks a law that conscience tells him is unjust,
and who willingly accepts the penalty of imprisonment in order to
arouse the conscience of the community over its injustice,
is in reality expressing the highest respect for the law.

Dr. King is describing the time-honored concept of civil disobedience. During my research, I discovered that this sentiment goes back much further than Henry David Thoreau, who is most famous for advancing the idea. Indeed, the best articulation of the idea comes from a poet—one of the most famous of all time. Writing centuries before Dr. King, Thoreau, and Mahatma Gandhi violated laws they considered unjust, John Milton wrote in 1645:

> **Men of most renowned virtue have sometimes**
> **by transgressing most truly kept the law.**

Enlightened Europeans and Americans weren't the only people to recognize the value of openness to criticism. Well before Europeans settled in the New World, the Native Americans had a saying:

> **Your greatest enemy is your greatest friend.**

How can a great enemy be a great friend? It's easy. Your greatest enemies want you to fail. They want this so badly that they are highly motivated to discover your weaknesses and fatal flaws. But if you can go to school on your enemy's assessment of your weaknesses—and improve yourself by taking some appropriate countermeasures—then nobody is more valuable than an enemy.

The strongest governments—and by extension the strongest people—establish mechanisms to help them figure out what's going well and to change things that need changing. But when we start thinking about reform and reformers, we run directly into another paradoxical political truth, one reflected in an intriguing oxymoronic observation from the English writer William Hazlitt:

> **It is essential to the triumph of reform that it should never succeed.**

What Hazlitt is suggesting, I think, is that social and political reformers are most valuable when they criticize from the outside and are not part of the established order. When reformers succeed, ironically, their so-called reforms often become greater problems than the problems they were attempting to resolve. Prohibition is perhaps the best example in the American experience. As long as Prohibitionists were outside of power, they played a valuable role in reminding the larger society of the evils of alcohol. But when they finally succeeded in becoming part of the established order, it was a colossal failure. H. L. Mencken might have had the Prohibition experience in mind when he wrote:

The worst government is the most moral.

This is a provocative observation if there ever was one. Mencken explained himself by adding this further thought about government: "One composed of cynics is often very tolerant and humane. But when fanatics are on top, there is no limit to repression."

Our Founding Fathers recognized the problems associated with religious fanaticism and wisely crafted a new government with a clear separation of church and state. But they were still wary of the potential for harm from those attempting to do good. In a letter to Thomas Jefferson, John Adams wrote:

Power always thinks it has a great soul
and vast views beyond the comprehension of the weak;
and that it is doing God's service, when it is violating all His laws.

This observation reveals not only a suspicion of established power, but also an awareness of one of the great ironies in world history—people engaged in the worst wrongdoing are often convinced they're in the right. It's an old insight, but is frequently ignored when zealous citizens and government officials attempt to impose their enlightened views on the rest of us poor devils. It's not surprising, then, that many people feel a certain wariness in the presence of zealous do-gooders. As Henry David Thoreau once wrote:

> **If I knew that a man was coming to my house with the conscious design of doing me good, I should run for my life.**

The problem of government zealotry has also been recognized by the U.S. Supreme Court. In a 1928 opinion, Justice Louis Brandeis wrote:

> **Experience should teach us to be most on our guard to protect liberty when the government's purposes are beneficent . . . the greatest dangers to liberty lurk in insidious encroachment by men of zeal, well-meaning but without understanding.**

Even when people are right in trying to do good, they can fail by over-reaching, by attempting too much. This notion also goes back many centuries, to one of the Seven Wise Men of Greece. In establishing the new American government, Thomas Jefferson recalled the ancient insight:

> **We see the wisdom of Solon's remark, that no more good must be attempted than the nation can bear.**

It's the old oxymoronic theme of failing by trying to do too much. The nineteenth-century English statesman and historian Thomas Babington Macaulay applied the concept to the political arena when he wrote:

> **It may be laid as a universal rule that a government which attempts more than it ought will perform less.**

In less democratic countries, reformers often become revolutionaries, and revolutionaries sometimes succeed in toppling corrupt regimes. But when reformers take over the reins of power, the result is all too predictable. It's happened in Russia, China, Cuba, and myriad other countries. In the words of the political philosopher Hannah Arendt:

> **The most radical revolutionary will become
> a conservative the day after the revolution.**

On January 8, 1790, George Washington delivered an address to both houses of Congress. In that speech—which inaugurated the tradition of an annual State of the Union Address—Washington said:

> **To be prepared for war is one of
> the most effectual means of preserving peace.**

Washington's maxim has shaped U.S. policy ever since, with almost every American president echoing the sentiment. In an 1897 speech at the Naval War College, Theodore Roosevelt recalled Washington's quote and added:

> **Preparation for war is the surest guaranty for peace.**

A few other American presidents have piggybacked on Washington's quote and extended it in interesting ways:

> **We are going to have peace even if we have to fight for it.**
>
> DWIGHT D. EISENHOWER

> **I want peace and I'm willing to fight for it.**
>
> HARRY S TRUMAN

In that first address to Congress, Washington cited a fourth-century Roman military theorist as the original author of the sentiment. In *De Rei Militari*, an influential treatise on military strategy, Flavius Vegetius Renatus wrote:

He, therefore, who desires peace should prepare for war.

The original sentiment, however, can be traced to Aristotle, who, in the fourth century B.C., wrote in *Nichomachean Ethics:*

We make war that we may live in peace.

Not all examples of political oxymoronica are serious. Some are light-hearted looks at well-known political realities:

There's nothing so permanent as a temporary job in Washington.
GEORGE ALLEN

All politicians know that every "temporary" political initiative promised as a short-term poultice stays on the books forever.
CYNTHIA OZICK

Others appear nonsensical at first glance, but are really quite inspired:

We're going to move left and right at the same time.
JERRY BROWN

And some border on the brilliant:

The liberals can understand everything
but people who don't understand them.

LENNY BRUCE

We who are liberal and progressive know that the poor are our equals
in every sense except that of being equal to us.

LIONEL TRILLING

In the remainder of this chapter, let's take a look at more examples of
political oxymoronica.

A patriot must always be ready
to defend his country against its government.

EDWARD ABBEY

No oppression is so heavy or lasting as that which is
inflicted by the perversion and exorbitance of legal authority.

JOSEPH ADDISON

The main dangers in this life are
the people who want to change everything—or nothing.

NANCY ASTOR

Democracy means government by discussion,
but it is only effective if you can stop people talking.

CLEMENT ATLEE

It only takes a politician believing in what he says
for the others to stop believing in him.

JEAN BAUDRILLARD

In Israel, in order to be a realist you must believe in miracles.

DAVID BEN-GURION

The trouble in modern democracy is that men do not approach to
leadership until they have lost the desire to lead anyone.

LORD BEVERIDGE

Even in a declaration of war one observes the rules of politeness.

PRINCE OTTO VON BISMARCK

There are no persons capable of stooping so low
as those who desire to rise in the world.

LADY MARGUERITE BLESSINGTON

The heart of a statesman should be in his head.

NAPOLEON BONAPARTE

The most important thing we do is not doing.

LOUIS BRANDEIS, ON THE SUPREME COURT

Anybody that wants the presidency so much that he'll spend two years
organizing and campaigning for it is not to be trusted with the office.

DAVID S. BRODER

Mere parsimony is not economy . . . Expense, and great expense,
may be an essential part of true economy.

EDMUND BURKE

Liberty must be limited in order to be possessed.

EDMUND BURKE

Nothing turns out to be so oppressive and unjust
as a feeble government.

EDMUND BURKE

An honest politician is one who when he's bought stays bought.

SIMON CAMERON

English experience indicates that when two political parties
agree about something, it is generally wrong.

G. K. CHESTERTON

Nobody believes a rumor here in Washington
until it's officially denied.

EDWARD CHEYFITZ

My father has spent the best years of his life
writing his extemporaneous speeches.

RANDOLPH CHURCHILL, ON WINSTON CHURCHILL

I have always been a bit shy of the really extemporary speech
ever since I heard it said that an extemporary speech
was not worth the paper it was written on.

WINSTON CHURCHILL

I always avoid prophesying beforehand,
because it is a much better policy
to prophesy after the event has already taken place.

WINSTON CHURCHILL

We are in bondage to the law in order that we may be free.

CICERO (FIRST CENTURY B.C.)

War is much too serious a business to be entrusted to the military.

GEORGES CLEMENCEAU

In politics as in religion, it so happens that we have less charity
for those who believe the half of our creed,
than for those that deny the whole of it.

CHARLES CALEB COLTON

In order to become the master, the politician poses as the servant.

CHARLES DE GAULLE

I've got all my enemies in the cabinet
where I can keep an eye on them.

JOHN DIEFENBAKER

I must follow the people. Am I not their leader?

BENJAMIN DISRAELI

A proletarian dictatorship is never proletarian.

WILL AND ARIEL DURANT

Every form of government tends to perish
by an excess of its basic principles.

WILL DURANT

The greatest power available to man is not to use it.

MEISTER ECKHART

We must be strong militarily, but beyond a certain point
military strength can become a national weakness.

DWIGHT D. EISENHOWER

We were nosed out by a landslide.

MALCOLM S. FORBES, ON HIS DEFEAT IN A NEW YORK STATE

GUBERNATORIAL ELECTION

**Galbraith's law states that
anyone who says he won't resign four times, will.**

JOHN KENNETH GALBRAITH

**Those who insist on the dignity of their office
show they have not deserved it.**

BALTASAR GRACIÁN

**I know no method to secure the repeal of bad or obnoxious laws
so effective as their stringent execution.**

ULYSSES S. GRANT

I worry incessantly that I might be too clear.

ALAN GREENSPAN

**There is no surer way to misread any document
than to read it literally.**

LEARNED HAND, IN *GIUSEPPI V. WALLING* (1944)

**I have no trouble with my enemies. But my goddam friends . . .
they are the ones that keep me walking the floor nights.**

WARREN G. HARDING

I can with truth say mine is a situation of dignified slavery.

ANDREW JACKSON, ON THE PRESIDENCY

The second office of the government is honorable and easy,
the first is but a splendid misery.

THOMAS JEFFERSON, COMPARING THE VICE-PRESIDENCY
AND THE PRESIDENCY

Never did a prisoner, released from his chains,
feel such relief as I shall on shaking off the shackles of power.

THOMAS JEFFERSON, ON LEAVING THE PRESIDENCY

The true leader is always led.

CARL JUNG

Office hours are from twelve to one, with an hour off for lunch.

GEORGE S. KAUFMAN, ON THE U.S. SENATE

Mothers all want their sons to grow up to be President,
but they don't want them to become politicians in the process.

JOHN F. KENNEDY

The United States has to move very fast to even stand still.

JOHN F. KENNEDY

The more laws and order are made prominent,
the more thieves and robbers there will be.

LAO-TZU (SIXTH CENTURY B.C.)

The paradox of British politics:
The moment one appropriates power one becomes impotent.

RAMSEY MACDONALD

At 34, he fit the ironic description
of the quintessential Rhodes Scholar,
someone with a great future behind him.
DAVID MARANISS, ON BILL CLINTON AFTER HE BECAME
THE YOUNGEST GOVERNOR IN HISTORY
TO BE DEFEATED AFTER ONE TERM

The only thing that saves us from the bureaucracy is its inefficiency.
EUGENE MCCARTHY

If experience teaches us anything at all, it teaches us this:
that a good politician, under democracy,
is quite as unthinkable as an honest burglar.
H. L. MENCKEN

If you are sure you understand everything that is going on around you,
you are hopelessly confused.
WALTER MONDALE

If the laws could speak for themselves,
they would complain of lawyers in the first place.
CHARLES MONTAGU (LORD HALIFAX)

Anyone who deliberately tries to get himself elected to public office
is permanently disqualified from holding one.
SIR THOMAS MORE, IN *UTOPIA* (1516)

Liberal institutions straightway cease from being liberal
the moment they are soundly established.
FRIEDRICH NIETZSCHE

No TV performance takes such careful preparation
as an off-the-cuff talk.

RICHARD M. NIXON

The secret of rulership is to combine a belief in one's infallibility
with the power to learn from past mistakes.

GEORGE ORWELL

All propaganda is lies—even when it is telling the truth.

GEORGE ORWELL

The people have always some champion
whom they set over them and nurse into greatness. . . .
This and no other is the root from which a tyrant springs;
when he first appears he is a protector.

PLATO, IN *THE REPUBLIC*
(FOURTH CENTURY B.C.)

He who would rule must hear and be deaf, see and be blind.

PROVERB (GERMAN)

No one has a finer command of language
than the person who keeps his mouth shut.

SAM RAYBURN

You have got to prove your manhood down here
whether you're a man or a woman.

ANN RICHARDS, ON TEXAS POLITICS

The more you observe politics, the more you've got to admit
that each party is worse than the other.

WILL ROGERS

The South is dry and will vote dry.
That is, everybody sober enough to stagger to the polls will.

WILL ROGERS, DURING PROHIBITION

Poverty is an expensive luxury. We cannot afford it.

ELEANOR ROOSEVELT

It is only the warlike power of a civilized people
that can give peace to the world.

THEODORE ROOSEVELT

The great virtue of my radicalism lies in the fact that
I am perfectly ready, if necessary,
to be radical on the conservative side.

THEODORE ROOSEVELT

A fanatical belief in democracy
makes democratic institutions impossible.

BERTRAND RUSSELL

Every nation ridicules other nations, and all are right.

ARTHUR SCHOPENHAUER

All laws act in restraint of toleration,
even when they are laws to enforce toleration.

GEORGE BERNARD SHAW

All the ills of democracy can be cured by more democracy.

ALFRED E. SMITH

Sincere diplomacy is no more possible than dry water or wooded iron.

JOSEPH STALIN

The more complete the despotism,
the more smoothly all things move on the surface.

ELIZABETH CADY STANTON

The more corrupt the state, the more numerous the laws.

TACITUS (SECOND CENTURY A.D.)

There is nothing more tyrannical than a
strong popular feeling among a democratic people.

ANTHONY TROLLOPE

A phenomenon noticeable throughout history
regardless of place or period is the pursuit
by governments of policies contrary to their own interests.

BARBARA W. TUCHMAN

If you want to rise in politics in the United States there is
one subject you must stay away from, and that is politics.

GORE VIDAL

The Labour Party is going about the country stirring up apathy.

WILLIAM WHITELAW

The best politics that could happen for our republic
would be the abolition of politics.

WALT WHITMAN

Those who try to lead the people can only do so by following the mob.

OSCAR WILDE

I adore political parties.
They are the only place left to us where people don't talk politics.

OSCAR WILDE

If I am to speak for ten minutes, I need a week for preparation;
if fifteen minutes, three days; if half an hour, two days;
if an hour, I am ready now.

WOODROW WILSON

It is a fitting irony that under Richard Nixon,
launder became a dirty word.

WILLIAM ZINSSER

chapter seven

OXYMORONICA ON STAGE & SCREEN

During the eighteenth century, David Garrick was England's greatest actor. A man of enormous talent onstage, he could be imperious and full of himself offstage. While Garrick was enjoying his success, the Irish-born Oliver Goldsmith was emerging as one of England's most popular writers. When Goldsmith died in 1774, he had been working on a series of rhymed sketches called "Retaliations," in which he skewered the leading figures of the day. About Garrick he wrote:

> On the stage he was natural, simple, affecting;
> 'Twas only that when he was off he was acting.

It's a great oxymoronic insult, to be sure, but it also captures an important reality about the crazy world of show business, where contradictions and all kinds of topsy-turviness abound.

When successful actors describe their youth, many recall their teenage years as times of great shyness, sometimes even of great insecurity. It has almost become a cliché that, when many shy and insecure teens are introduced to acting and begin performing in their first roles, something special happens—they experience a sense of satisfaction and competence that has not been present in their regular lives. It's called "the acting bug" for good reason. Those magical moments onstage not only dull some of the pain of adolescence, they also provide young actors with an opportunity to find a new way of being in the world. In her 1986 autobiography, *One More Time*, Carol Burnett captured this scenario perfectly when she wrote about her high school acting experiences:

I liked myself better when I wasn't me.

The actress Geena Davis also noticed the irony that so many introverted people have been attracted to such an outgoing profession:

It's a weird dichotomy.
So many of us are shy, and then we end up becoming actors.
We're shy exhibitionists.

Once young actors succumb to the acting bug, they strive to learn their craft, focusing on things like memorizing lines and enunciating them clearly. But many young thespians don't discover until much later an important paradoxical truth about acting:

Good actors are good because of things they tell us without talking.
When they are talking, they are the servants of the dramatist.
It is what they can show the audience when they are not talking
that reveals the fine actor.

SIR CEDRIC HARDWICKE

The great director Alfred Hitchcock said the same thing more succinctly:

> **The best screen actor is the man**
> **who can do nothing extremely well.**

When acting is done extremely well, the effect on an audience is almost magical. Transfixed by what they are seeing on stage, audience members achieve a state known as "the suspension of disbelief." In plain English, this means they forget they're witnessing a performance and believe they are seeing something real. Of course, acting is not the real thing, it's a performance. So how do actors become so convincing and so believable that theatergoers suspend their disbelief? Two of Hollywood's most famous names have been credited with virtually the same tongue-in-cheek answer:

> **Acting is all about honesty.**
> **If you can fake that, you've got it made.**
>
> GEORGE BURNS

> **I once asked Barbara Stanwyck the secret of acting.**
> **She said: "Just be truthful—**
> **and if you can fake that, you've got it made."**
>
> FRED MACMURRAY

The actress Glenda Jackson offered a more serious answer, but said pretty much the same thing:

> **The whole essence of learning lines is to forget them**
> **so you can make them sound like**
> **you thought of them that instant.**

And the British comedian Benny Hill summed it all up in a neat oxymoron:

> **That's what show business is—sincere insincerity.**

Of course, actors have real lives as well as screen lives, and fascinating oxymoronic elements have emerged in that arena as well. A few years back, Marlon Brando and George C. Scott were nominated for Academy Awards. Both were opposed to such ceremonies and held press conferences to announce that they would not accept any awards. The witty British actor Peter Ustinov, sensing a paradox in the public nature of their refusals, observed:

> **To refuse awards ... is another way of accepting them**
> **with more noise than is normal.**

Great oxymoronic observations about the world of show business don't come only from actors and actresses. A 1987 *Variety* article reported on a "Young Artists" seminar, in which veterans of the film business talked about the industry to newcomers. Producer Tony Bill shared this thought:

> **The history of success in our business is rejection ...**
> **And the history of failure is "the sure thing."**

Bill was describing a well-known paradox in the film world. Almost every successful film in Hollywood history was originally rejected—often many times—by directors, actors, studios, and producers. And, of course, the reverse was also true: Dubbing a project "a sure thing" was tantamount to giving it the kiss of death.

Great oxymoronic lines are often crafted by playwrights and screenwriters, inserted into their productions, and eventually delivered by actors. In fact, many of the quotes attributed in these pages to Oscar Wilde and George Bernard Shaw come from their plays, not their essays or other writings. Here are a few more examples from these two great writers, all first delivered to the world by actors on the London stage. The first batch comes from Wilde:

> **When the gods wish to punish us they answer our prayers.**
>
> *AN IDEAL HUSBAND* (1895)

> **The only difference between a caprice and a lifelong passion is that the caprice lasts a little longer.**
>
> *THE PICTURE OF DORIAN GRAY* (1891)

> **I can resist everything except temptation.**
>
> *LADY WINDERMERE'S FAN* (1891)

And these come from Shaw:

> **How conventional all you unconventional people are!**
>
> *CANDIDA* (1897)

> **A lifetime of happiness! No man alive could bear it; it would be hell on earth.**
>
> *MAN AND SUPERMAN* (1903)

> **You have learnt something. That always feels at first as if you had lost something.**
>
> *MAJOR BARBARA* (1905)

The greatest playwright of all time also inserted numerous oxymoronic lines in his plays. Other examples of Shakespearian oxymoronica appear throughout the book, but here are several that were heard for the first time by theatergoing audiences four centuries ago:

> **Unbidden guests**
> **Are often welcomest when they are gone.**
>
> *KING HENRY THE SIXTH, PART ONE*

> **If thou art rich, thou art poor.**
>
> *MEASURE FOR MEASURE*

> **The more I give to thee,**
> **The more I have.**
>
> *ROMEO AND JULIET*

> **This fellow's wise enough to play the fool,**
> **And to do that well craves a kind of wit.**
>
> *TWELFTH-NIGHT*

The world of show business is filled with some of the most interesting and flamboyant characters the world has ever seen. David Bowie, a pretty fair actor as well as a legendary musician, has been known for his sensational stage costumes. When someone once asked him why he chose to wear a dress, he replied:

> **You must understand that this is not**
> **a woman's dress I'm wearing. It's a man's dress.**

Bowie was clearly aware of the oxymoronic nature of his remark. But, as you will see in a later chapter, some wonderful oxymoronic quotes come about by accident. Many have come from Hollywood legends, like Samuel Goldwyn:

We pay him too much, but he's worth it.

It's an impossible situation, but it has possibilities.

The director Michael Curtiz spoke a broken English that also resulted in some pretty amazing locutions. About a musical he directed, he once said:

It's dull from beginning to end. But it's loaded with entertainment.

We'll examine more examples of "inadvertent oxymoronica" a little later in the book. In the remainder of this chapter, though, let's take a look at more quite deliberate oxymoronic creations, all from the world of stage and screen.

You can make a killing in the theater, but not a living.
ROBERT ANDERSON

Definition of tragedy: A hero destroyed by the excess of his virtues.
ARISTOTLE (FOURTH CENTURY B.C.)

Some of the biggest failures I ever had were successes.
PEARL BAILEY

I wasn't really naked. I simply didn't have any clothes on.
JOSEPHINE BAKER

**In the theatre the audience want to be surprised—
but by things they expect.**
TRISTAN BERNARD

I just want to be normally insane.

MARLON BRANDO

Tragedy is if I cut my finger.
Comedy is if I walk into an open sewer and die.

MEL BROOKS

Comedy is tragedy plus time.

CAROL BURNETT

When I played drunks I had to remain sober
because I didn't know how to play them when I was drunk.

RICHARD BURTON

It takes twenty years to make an overnight success.

EDDIE CANTOR

The most difficult character in comedy is that of the fool,
and he must be no simpleton that plays the part.

MIGUEL DE CERVANTES

What a sad business is being funny!

CHARLES CHAPLIN, IN THE 1952 FILM *LIMELIGHT*

I can take any amount of criticism, so long as it is unqualified praise.

NOEL COWARD

What acting really is, is pretending—
while you're pretending you're not pretending.

TED DANSON

Being a star has made it possible for me to get insulted in places
where the average Negro could never hope to get insulted.

SAMMY DAVIS JR.

I'm not afraid to show my feminine side—
it's part of what makes me a man.

GERARD DEPARDIEU

Catherine Deneuve is the man I've always wanted to be.

GERARD DEPARDIEU

After my screen test, the director clapped his hands gleefully
and yelled, "She can't talk! She can't act! She's sensational!"

AVA GARDNER

Black and white are the most ravishing colors of all in film.

PENELOPE GILLIATT

As far as the filmmaking process is concerned,
stars are essentially worthless—and absolutely essential.

WILLIAM GOLDMAN

All my shows are great. Some of them are bad. But they are all great.

LEW GRADE

When people tell you how young you look,
they are telling you how old you are.

CARY GRANT

Work can only be universal
if it is rooted in a part of its creator
which is most privately and particularly himself.

TYRONE GUTHRIE

I'm now at the age where I've got to prove
that I'm just as good as I never was.

REX HARRISON

That look of threatening benevolence.

MOSS HART, ON FIRST-NIGHT PRODUCTIONS

Stardom can be a gilded slavery.

HELEN HAYES

Actors are the only honest hypocrites.

WILLIAM HAZLITT

Give them pleasure—the same pleasure they have
when they wake up from a nightmare.

ALFRED HITCHCOCK, ON AUDIENCES

Acting provides the fulfillment of never being fulfilled.

GLENDA JACKSON

The important thing in acting is to be able to laugh and cry.
If I have to cry, I think of my sex life.
If I have to laugh, I think of my sex life.

GLENDA JACKSON

We believe . . . that the applause of silence
is the only kind that counts.

ALFRED JARRY

I sat screaming silently.

PAULINE KAEL, ON THE 1991 FILM *THE SILENCE OF THE LAMBS*

I'm no actor, and I have sixty-four pictures to prove it.

VICTOR MATURE

Opening night: the night before the play is ready to open.

GEORGE JEAN NATHAN

My mom never saw the irony in calling me a sonofabitch.

JACK NICHOLSON

There is no sincerity like a woman telling a lie.

CECIL PARKER, IN THE 1958 FILM *INDISCREET*

I was a 14-year-old boy for 30 years.

MICKEY ROONEY, ON HIS FILM ROLES

When I was 14, I was the oldest I ever was . . .
I've been getting younger ever since.

SHIRLEY TEMPLE

A good drama critic is one who perceives
what is happening in the theatre of his time.
A great drama critic also perceives what is *not* happening.

KENNETH TYNAN

Comedy is simply a funny way of being serious.

PETER USTINOV

Good bad taste is always fueled by rage and anger
with humor thrown in.
Bad bad taste is fueled by stupidity and ignorance,
and it comes out as anger.

JOHN WATERS

These girls in love never realize they should be honestly dishonest
instead of being dishonestly honest.

CLIFTON WEBB, IN THE 1954 FILM *THREE COINS*

IN THE FOUNTAIN

I love acting. It is so much more real than life.

OSCAR WILDE

Don't be too clever for an audience. Make it obvious.
Make the subtleties obvious also.

BILLY WILDER

Every now and then when you're on stage,
you can hear the best sound that a player can hear.
It is a sound you can't get in movies or in television.
It is the sound of a wonderful, deep silence
that means you've hit them where they live.

SHELLEY WINTERS

chapter eight

ARTISTIC OXYMORONICA

The creativity of people in the world of the fine arts is not restricted to their artistic creations; it also shows up in the language they use to describe the work they do and the world in which they live. Pablo Picasso, a genius with words as well as other media, crafted many remarkable lines in his lifetime. One of his best was:

We all know that Art is not truth.
Art is a lie that makes us realize truth.

In this provocative paradoxical observation, Picasso points out that artists don't create reality; they only try to capture it through their contrived—and ultimately artificial—creations. When works of art help art lovers arrive at a deeper truth or a more profound understanding, these fabrications—these artistic lies—help people get to a place they might never have arrived at on their own.

Picasso is not the only person in art history to link the false and the true in this manner. Many other great artists have expressed similar thoughts:

In painting you must give the idea of the true by means of the false.

EDGAR DEGAS

Of all lies, art is the least untrue.

GUSTAVE FLAUBERT

The matters I relate
Are true lies.

JEAN COCTEAU

Lying, the telling of beautiful untrue things,
is the proper aim of art.

OSCAR WILDE

Picasso added an important corollary to his famous observation that art is a lie that helps people realize the truth:

The artist must know the manner whereby
to convince others of the truthfulness of his lies.

His point here is that it takes great talent for artists to make sure their contrivances don't look like contrivances. In other words, artists can succeed only if their lies look truthful. Over the years, many creative thinkers have made the same point—to succeed, art must not look like art:

**The most subtle art, the strongest and deepest art—supreme art—
is the one that does not at first allow itself to be recognized.**

ANDRÉ GIDE

The height of art is to conceal art.

QUINTILIAN

The highest condition of art is artlessness.

HENRY DAVID THOREAU

Artistic creation is much more than a productive form of lying. It's also about dreaming. In a 1986 *Time* magazine article, Andrew Wyeth said:

I do more painting when I'm not painting.

How can people paint when they're not painting? Wyeth clarified matters when he explained that he dreams all the time, and often paints images in his subconscious. Paul Gauguin said pretty much the same thing in these words:

I shut my eyes in order to see.

Both observations suggest that the most important creative work occurs when artists are not in production mode, but when they're far away from their studios—thinking and visualizing, or even dreaming. Vincent van Gogh used another great literary device—chiasmus—to describe the creative process:

**First I dream my painting,
then I paint my dream.**

Musical artists have also found oxymoronic phrasing helpful in describing elements of their craft. Advancing the notion that art must avoid looking like art, the legendary Duke Ellington once said:

> **The artist must say it without saying it.**

Other musicians have reminded us of a related paradoxical truth—great performances come not from what artists are playing, but what they're not playing. The great Miles Davis said:

> **Don't play what's there, play what's not there.**

The Austrian pianist and composer Artur Schnabel said it this way:

> **The notes I handle no better than many pianists.**
> **But the pauses between the notes—ah, that is where the art resides.**

Other artistic geniuses have also joined in the oxymoronic act. Martha Graham, a pioneering figure in the world of modern dance, put her finger on the motivation of all creative people when she observed:

> **No artist is pleased . . .**
> **There is only a queer divine dissatisfaction,**
> **a blessed unrest that keeps us marching**
> **and makes us more alive than the others.**

Artists in the film world have also been guided by important paradoxical insights. In an interview several years ago, filmmaker David Cronenberg touched on the subject of artistic responsibility. After agreeing that the duty of adults is to be responsible, he added:

> **But as an artist, that's where the paradox is—**
> **your responsibility is to be irresponsible.**

Cronenberg found a clever new way of expressing an old truth—an important responsibility of the artist is to challenge social conventions and to question traditional modes of thinking. He added, "As soon as you talk about social or political responsibility, you've amputated the best limbs you've got as an artist."

Critics, writers, and even art administrators have also contributed some memorable examples of artistic oxymoronica. John Ruskin, the influential nineteenth-century English art critic, observed:

An artist should be fit for the best society and keep out of it.

The French writer Françoise Sagan said almost everything that needs to be said about the essence of jazz when she wrote:

Jazz music is an intensified feeling of nonchalance.

And in a 1986 story in *Time* magazine, Françoise Cachin, director of Paris's *Musée d'Orsay*, said of the museum's collection:

Certainly we have bad paintings.
We have only the "greatest" bad paintings.

When creative artists have ventured into the language arena, many have been drawn to the allure of oxymoronic phrasing, crafting some highly original—even remarkable—observations in the process. Let's take a look at more examples of artistic oxymoronica in the remainder of this chapter.

The creative person is both more primitive and more cultivated . . .
a lot madder and a lot saner, than the average person.
FRANK BARRON

To study music, we must learn the rules.
To create music, we must forget them.

NADIA BOULANGER

The responsibility of the artist consists in perfecting his work
so that it may become attractively disinteresting.

JOHN CAGE

What I say to an artist is, *When you can't paint—paint.*

JOYCE CARY

The most perfect technique is that which is not noticed at all.

PABLO CASALS

An original artist is unable to copy.
So he has only to copy in order to be original.

JEAN COCTEAU

Jazz is the only music in which the same note
can be played night after night but differently each time.

ORNETTE COLEMAN

Only when he no longer knows what he is doing
does the painter do good things.

EDGAR DEGAS

An artist is forced by others to paint out of his own free will.

WILLEM DE KOONING

Experience has two things to teach;
the first is that we must correct a great deal;
the second, that we must not correct too much.

EUGÈNE DELACROIX, ON FINISHING A PAINTING

One always has to spoil a picture a little bit, in order to finish it.

EUGÈNE DELACROIX

What delights us in visible beauty is the invisible.

MARIE VON EBNER-ESCHENBACH

In art the best is good enough.

JOHANN WOLFGANG VON GOETHE

The artist has a twofold relation to nature;
he is at once her master and her slave.

JOHANN WOLFGANG VON GOETHE

My aim in painting has always been the most exact transcription
possible of my most intimate impression of nature.

EDWARD HOPPER

Perfection itself is imperfection.

VLADIMIR HOROWITZ

When people hear good music, it makes them homesick
for something they never had, and never will have.

EDGAR WATSON HOWE

Music expresses that which cannot be said
and on which it is impossible to be silent.

VICTOR HUGO

What is called a sincere work is one that is
endowed with enough strength to give reality to an illusion.

MAX JACOB

The more minimal the art,
the more maximum the explanation.

HILTON KRAMER

What is best in music is not to be found in the notes.

GUSTAV MAHLER

You can only make art that talks to the masses
when you have nothing to say to them.

ANDRÉ MALRAUX

Art teaches nothing, except the significance of life.

HENRY MILLER

Being an artist means ceasing to take seriously
that very serious person we are when we are not an artist.

JOSÉ ORTEGA Y GASSET

Nothing is more useful to man than
those arts which have no utility.

OVID (FIRST CENTURY B.C.)

How vain is painting, which is admired for reproducing
the likeness of things whose originals are not admired.

BLAISE PASCAL

What is left out of a work of art is as important as,
if not more important than, what is put in.

KATHERINE PATERSON

All works of art should begin . . . at the end.

EDGAR ALLAN POE

Art is too serious to be taken seriously.

AD REINHARDT

Art is . . . the reasoned derangement of the senses.

KENNETH REXROTH

Art, whose honesty must work through artifice,
cannot avoid cheating truth.

LAURA RIDING

Artists—by definition innocent—don't steal.
But they do borrow without giving back.

NED ROREM

Music is the sole art which evokes nostalgia for the future.

NED ROREM

It is only with the heart that one can see rightly;
what is essential is invisible to the eye.

ANTOINE DE SAINT-EXUPÉRY

When I don't like a piece of music,
I make a point of listening to it more closely.

FLORENT SCHMITT

The sonatas of Mozart are unique;
they are too easy for children, and too difficult for adults.

ARTUR SCHNABEL

My compositions spring from my sorrows.
Those that give the world the greatest delight
were born of my deepest griefs.

FRANZ SCHUBERT

The theory that music has a depraving effect on morals
has now been abandoned to the old women of both sexes.

GEORGE BERNARD SHAW

Offensive objects, at a proper distance,
acquire even a degree of beauty.

WILLIAM SHENSTONE

What an artist is for is to tell us what we see
but do not know that we see.

EDITH SITWELL

Sleep is an excellent way of listening to an opera.

JAMES STEPHENS

Too many pieces of music finish too long after the end.

IGOR STRAVINSKY

It always strikes me, and it is very peculiar, that, whenever
we see the image of indescribable and unutterable desolation—
of loneliness, poverty, and misery, the end and extreme of things—
the thought of God comes into one's mind.

VINCENT VAN GOGH

A work of art has an author, and yet, when it is perfect,
it has something which is essentially anonymous about it.

SIMONE WEIL

To reveal art and conceal the artist is art's aim.

OSCAR WILDE

This is the most autobiographical song I've ever written.
I'm thankful I had the presence of mind never to put any words to it.
BENNETT WILLIAMS, INTRODUCING AN INSTRUMENTAL SONG

It looks wrong, and it sounds wrong, but it's right.
RALPH VAUGHAN WILLIAMS, ON A PASSAGE FROM HIS
FOURTH SYMPHONY

chapter nine

OXYMORONIC INSULTS
(AND A FEW COMPLIMENTS)

Sigmund Freud once remarked that the person who hurled the first insult instead of a rock made the first real step toward civilization. It was an important first step, to be sure, but I'll bet those early insults were pretty primitive. Indeed, the preponderance of insults delivered even today are quite crude. But every now and then, a zinger is hurled with such panache that even the recipient is likely to be impressed. That might have happened when Henry James said of George Eliot:

> She is magnificently ugly—deliciously hideous . . .
> Now in this vast ugliness resides a most powerful beauty
> which, in a very few minutes, steals forth and charms the mind.

Picking up on Freud's earlier comment, it's possible to argue that one of the hallmarks of a civilized society is the sophistication of the insults that its citizens hurl at one another. The Romans, who prided themselves on being ultrasophisticated, were most favorably impressed when one of their numbers would skewer a victim with wit and a clever turn of phrase. In the second century B.C., the Roman poet Terence didn't disappoint the folks in the gallery when he observed about a contemporary woman:

> **She never was really charming till she died.**

Terence's remark about the recently departed woman brings to mind a famous anecdote about Voltaire. Informed that a writer he hated had recently died, Voltaire was urged to publicly express his condolences and say some words in honor of the man. His remark simply enhanced his reputation as one of France's greatest wits:

> **I have just been informed that Monsieur _____ is dead.**
> **He was a staunch patriot, a talented writer,**
> **a loyal friend, a devoted husband and father—**
> **provided he is really dead.**

Oxymoronic insults have been delivered with deadly precision throughout history. In his 1643 book of reflections, *Religio Medici*, Sir Thomas Browne wrote:

> **Diogenes I hold to be the most vainglorious man of his time,**
> **and more ambitious, in refusing all honors,**
> **than Alexander in rejecting none.**

Browne's observation reflects an interesting fact about human beings, who can be proud of their humility and oh-so-public in their rejection of honors. Tom Stoppard observed this tendency in James Joyce, writing that he was:

**An essentially private man who wished his
total indifference to public notice to be universally recognized.**

The English, with their characteristic wryness, have shown a special penchant for oxymoronic insults. After reading the memoirs of Field Marshall Douglas Haig, the commander of the ill-fated British Expeditionary Force in World War I, Lord Beaverbrook said:

> **With the publication of his private papers in 1952,
> he committed suicide 25 years after his death.**

And writing about one of England's least memorable prime ministers—Sir Henry Campbell-Bannerman—the English writer Nicolas Bentley wrote in his 1974 *An Edwardian Album*:

> **He is remembered chiefly as
> the man about whom all is forgotten.**

The German composer Richard Wagner holds the unique distinction of being the object of three memorable oxymoronic insults—from three of history's most famous wits:

> **I love Wagner, but the music I prefer
> is that of a cat hung up by its tail outside a window
> and trying to stick to panes of glass with its claws.**
> CHARLES BAUDELAIRE

> **The late Bill Nye once said,
> "I have been told that Wagner's music
> is better than it sounds."**
> MARK TWAIN

I like Wagner's music better than anybody's.
It is so loud that one can talk the whole time
without other people hearing what one says.

OSCAR WILDE

Some of the best critical remarks—insults if you will—are not directed toward people, but entire fields of human endeavor:

It seems a pity that psychology should have
destroyed all our knowledge of human nature.

G. K. CHESTERTON

Psychoanalysis is the disease it purports to cure.

KARL KRAUS

But it is nations and nationalities that have been the targets of the most maliciously witty insults. Many have been aimed at Ireland and the Irish:

The problem with Ireland is that it's a country full of genius,
but with absolutely no talent.

HUGH LEONARD

The Irish don't know what they want
and are prepared to fight to the death to get it.

SIDNEY LITTLEWOOD

A fighting race who never won a battle . . .
a pious race excelling in blasphemy . . .
who sing of love and practice fratricide . . .
with a harp for an emblem and no musicians . . .
whose tongue is silver and whose heart is black.

TOM PENHALIGON

The English have also been targeted:

> **The English instinctively admire any man**
> **who has no talent and is modest about it.**
>
> JAMES AGATE

> **I like the English.**
> **They have the most rigid code of immorality in the world.**
>
> MALCOLM BRADBURY

> **An Englishman, even if he is alone,**
> **forms an orderly queue of one.**
>
> GEORGE MIKES

> **The people of England are never so happy**
> **as when you tell them they are ruined.**
>
> ARTHUR MURPHY

> **The English have an extraordinary ability**
> **for flying into a great calm.**
>
> ALEXANDER WOOLLCOTT

I even found a trenchant 1799 observation about the Germans (one strikingly similar to a popular comment made about the Japanese in more recent times):

> **The German's special forte is original work**
> **in fields wherein others have prepared the way.**
> **He possesses in a superlative degree**
> **the art of being original by imitation.**
>
> G. C. LICHTENBERG

Oxymoronic compliments are far less common than oxymoronic insults, but they can be equally compelling. The French have long said of their Foreign Legion:

> **They were never defeated,**
> **they were only killed.**

And in one of the cleverest things ever written about the physical assets of Marilyn Monroe, Constance Bennett said upon first meeting the young ingénue:

> **There's a broad with her future behind her.**

Occasionally, it's hard to know whether an oxymoronic observation is critical or laudatory. A 1937 *Time* magazine review of one of John Steinbeck's best-known books offered this tantalizing observation:

> **An oxymoronic combination of the tough and tender,**
> ***Of Mice and Men* will appeal to**
> **sentimental cynics, cynical sentimentalists.**

There's an element of unexpectedness—even surprise—built into the structure of oxymoronic observations, making them particularly well suited for the delivery of devastating insults and, occasionally, compelling compliments. In the remainder of this chapter, you'll find examples of both.

> **Deep down, he's shallow.**
>
> ANONYMOUS

> **It was one of those plays in which all the actors**
> **unfortunately enunciated very clearly.**
>
> ROBERT C. BENCHLEY

He's the kind of guy who can brighten a room by leaving it.

MILTON BERLE, ON A CONTEMPORARY

He had nothing to say and he said it.

AMBROSE BIERCE, ON A CONTEMPORARY

Carlyle's eye was a terrible organ; he saw everything.

AUGUSTINE BIRRELL, ON THOMAS CARLYLE

Talleyrand is a silk stocking filled with mud.

NAPOLEON BONAPARTE

The cunning old codger knows that no emphasis
often constitutes the most powerful emphasis of all.

CLEANTH BROOKS, ON ROBERT FROST

Handel is so great and so simple that no one but
a professional musician is unable to understand him.

SAMUEL BUTLER

Mrs. P. had only one fault; she was perfect.
Otherwise, she was perfect.

TRUMAN CAPOTE, ON AN ACQUAINTANCE

The British government is a strange paradox, decided only to be
undecided, resolved to be irresolute, adamant for drift,
solid for fluidity, all-powerful to be impotent.

WINSTON CHURCHILL, ON STANLEY BALDWIN'S POLICIES
IN 1936

An empty taxi arrived at 10 Downing Street,
and when the door was opened Clement Atlee got out.

WINSTON CHURCHILL

Ryan O'Neal is so stiff and clumsy that he can't even manage
a part requiring him to be stiff and clumsy.

JAY COCKS

He has the manner of a giant with the look of a child,
a lazy activeness, a mad wisdom,
a solitude encompassing the world.

JEAN COCTEAU, ON ORSON WELLES

He has not a single redeeming defect.

BENJAMIN DISRAELI, ON WILLIAM GLADSTONE

He is just about the nastiest little man I've ever known.
He struts sitting down.

LILLIAN K. DYKSTRA, ON THOMAS DEWEY

Henry James was one of the nicest old ladies I ever met.

WILLIAM FAULKNER

He has impeccable bad taste.

OTIS FERGUSON, ON A CONTEMPORARY PLAYWRIGHT

A portrait endowed with every merit
excepting that of likeness to the original.

EDWARD GIBBON, ON ALEXANDER POPE'S
TRANSLATION OF HOMER

If it were better, it wouldn't be as good.

BRENDAN GILL, ON THE PLAY *BUTTERFLIES ARE FREE*

Venice would be a fine city if it were only drained.

ULYSSES S. GRANT, DURING VISIT TO VENICE IN 1879

She's genuinely bogus.
CHRISTOPHER HASSALL, ON DAME EDITH SITWELL

I learned an awful lot from him by doing the opposite.
HOWARD HAWKES, ON CECIL B. DE MILLE

Berlioz says nothing in his music but he says it magnificently.
JAMES GIBBONS HUNEKER, ON HECTOR BERLIOZ

A corpulent Adonis of fifty.
LEIGH HUNT, ON THE PRINCE REGENT (LATER GEORGE IV)

The perfection of rottenness.
WILLIAM JAMES, ON GEORGE SANTAYANA

I've just spent an hour talking to Tallulah for a few minutes.
FRED KEATING, ON TALLULAH BANKHEAD

***Hook and Ladder* is the sort of play that gives failures a bad name.**
WALTER KERR

He has delusions of adequacy.
WALTER KERR, ON A CONTEMPORARY ACTOR

When he's alone in a room, there's nobody there.
JOHN MAYNARD KEYNES, ON DAVID LLOYD GEORGE

**I have a thorough aversion to his character,
and a very moderate admiration of his genius;
he is great in so little a way.**
CHARLES LAMB, ON LORD BYRON

This is the most exciting place in the world to live.
There are so many ways to die here.

DENIS LEARY, ON NEW YORK CITY

Leonard Bernstein has been disclosing musical secrets
that have been well known for over 400 years.

OSCAR LEVANT

Oscar Wilde was a mixture of an Apollo and a monster.

GEORGE MEREDITH

He speaks English with the flawless imperfection of a New Yorker.

GILBERT MILLSTEIN, ON ANDRE SURMAIN

He was a most disagreeable companion . . .
His conversation was a procession of one.

FLORENCE NIGHTINGALE, ON THOMAS BABINGTON MACAULAY

The great thing about Errol was that
you knew precisely where you were with him—
because he always let you down.

DAVID NIVEN, ON ERROL FLYNN

The main thing that endears the United Nations
to member governments, and so enables it to survive,
is its proven capacity to fail.
You can safely appeal to the United Nations
in the comfortable certainty that it will let you down.

CONOR CRUISE O'BRIEN

A professional amateur.

LAURENCE OLIVIER, ON MARILYN MONROE

His leprosy is so perfect that men call him clean.
COVENTRY PATMORE, ON WILLIAM GLADSTONE

The man was a major comedian,
which is to say that he had the compassion of an icicle,
the effrontery of a carnival shill,
and the generosity of a pawnbroker.
S. J. PERELMAN, ON GROUCHO MARX

He inherited some good instincts from his Quaker forebears,
but by diligent hard work, he overcame them.
JAMES RESTON, ON RICHARD NIXON

How wonderful opera would be if there were no singers.
GIOACCHINO ANTONIO ROSSINI

Hoffer, our resident Peasant Philosopher,
is an example of articulate ignorance.
JOHN SEELYE, ON ERIC HOFFER

It is greatly to Mrs. Patrick Campbell's credit that, bad as the play was,
her acting was worse. It was a masterpiece of failure.
GEORGE BERNARD SHAW, REVIEWING *FEDORA* IN 1895

The chorus did everything to perfection except sing.
GEORGE BERNARD SHAW, IN AN 1889 REVIEW

I like him and his wife. He is so ladylike,
and she is such a perfect gentleman.
SYDNEY SMITH, ON AN UNNAMED COUPLE

People sometimes divide others into
those you laugh at and those you laugh with.
The young Auden was someone you could laugh-at-with.

STEPHEN SPENDER, ON W. H. AUDEN

She is such a good friend that she would throw all her acquaintances
into the water for the pleasure of fishing them out.

CHARLES-MAURICE DE TALLEYRAND, ON GERMAINE DE STAËL

When there is nothing whatever to say,
no one knows better than Mr. Milne how to say it.

THE LONDON TIMES, ABOUT A. A. MILNE IN 1937

A genius with the IQ of a moron.

GORE VIDAL, ON ANDY WARHOL

This agglomeration which was called and which still calls itself
the Holy Roman Empire is neither holy, nor Roman, nor an Empire.

VOLTAIRE

An inspired idiot.

HORACE WALPOLE, ON OLIVER GOLDSMITH

He's the kind of man a woman would have to marry to get rid of.

MAE WEST, ON A FELLOW ACTOR

He has a face like a hoosier Michael Angelo, so awful ugly
it becomes beautiful, with its strange mouth, its deep-cut,
criss-cross lines, and its doughnut complexion.

WALT WHITMAN, ON ABRAHAM LINCOLN

George Moore wrote brilliant English until he discovered grammar.

OSCAR WILDE

A sweetly vicious old lady.

TENNESSEE WILLIAMS, ON TRUMAN CAPOTE

There is absolutely nothing wrong with Oscar Levant
that a miracle couldn't fix.

ALEXANDER WOOLLCOTT

The nicest thing I can say about Frances Farmer
is that she is unbearable.

WILLIAM WYLER

chapter ten

OXYMORONIC ADVICE

There are few subjects in life more rife with paradoxical elements than the giving and receiving of advice. People ask for advice when they don't want it. They advise others to do things they rarely (or never) do themselves. And in a fascinating twist, people sometimes fare best when they do the opposite of what they're advised to do. George Bernard Shaw captured the confounding nature of the subject when he wrote:

Never take anybody's advice.

By giving advice and telling people to shun advice at the same time, Shaw puts recipients of his message in a strange position. Self-contradictory messages like this have always been of special interest to psychologists. A classic example is the admonition:

Be spontaneous.

There's no way out of the dilemma created by these words. If you follow the instructions, you're not being spontaneous. If you ignore the instructions and do nothing, you're not being spontaneous. Messages like this put people into what is called a "double-bind." For many years, psychologists believed that communication of this sort—when it occurred in families—contributed to the development of schizophrenia. Among linguaphiles, however, these kinds of verbal constructions have long been a source of great fun:

> **I always advise people never to give advice.**
>
> P. G. WODEHOUSE

> **Shun advice at any price—**
> **that's what I call good advice.**
>
> PIET HEIN

When most people ask for advice, the truth is they usually don't want advice per se, but some kind of approval for a course of action already decided on. Erica Jong said it this way in her 1977 book *How to Save Your Own Life:*

> **Advice is what we ask for when we**
> **already know the answer but wish we didn't.**

A century earlier, the American humorist Henry Wheeler Shaw, writing under the pen name Josh Billings, said pretty much the same thing:

> **Most people when they come to you for advice**
> **come to have their own opinions strengthened, not corrected.**

Even when people decide to follow advice, it's often not the wisest decision. Indeed, over the years many people have adopted what might be called a contrarian approach—seek advice and ignore it. A number of well-known people have described this strategy:

> I owe my success to having listened respectfully to the very best advice, and then going away and doing the exact opposite.
>
> G. K. CHESTERTON

> Listen carefully to first criticisms of your work. Note just what it is about your work the critics don't like—then cultivate it. That's the part of your work that's individual and worth keeping.
>
> JEAN COCTEAU

> I am glad that I paid so little attention to good advice; had I abided by it I might have been saved from some of my most valuable mistakes.
>
> GENE FOWLER

> If someone gives you so-called good advice, do the opposite; you can be sure it will be the right thing nine out of ten times.
>
> ANSELM FEUERBACH

> Always listen to experts. They'll tell you what can't be done and why. Then do it.
>
> ROBERT A. HEINLEIN

> Please give me some good advice in your next letter. I promise not to follow it.
>
> EDNA SAINT VINCENT MILLAY

Perhaps the most fascinating variation on the theme of oxymoronic advice is to advise people to do something, but to phrase the advice in a way that runs counter to the advice you're giving. An early precursor of this kind of message comes from the legendary trial attorney Clarence Darrow, who once said:

> **Even if you do learn to speak correct English,**
> **whom are you going to speak it to?**

You employed this strategy as a schoolchild if you ever said anything like "Don't use no double negatives" or "It ain't correct to say ain't." The best-known examples of this kind of lighthearted advice come from the language maven William Safire, who originally referred to them as "perverse rules of grammar" and eventually as "fumblerules." In 1979, Safire published three such rules in his "On Language" column in the *New York Times* and solicited other examples from his readers. Very quickly, language lovers around the world joined in the paradoxical fun of laying out a rule and violating it at the same time. I've seen scores of examples over the years, but here are a few of my favorites:

> **Never use a long word when a diminutive one will suffice.**

> **If I've told you once, I've told you a thousand times: Resist hyperbole.**

> **Eschew obfuscation.**

> **Avoid awkward or affected alliteration.**

> **Last, but not least, avoid clichés like the plague.**

Some of the best oxymoronic advice is of a counterintuitive nature, meaning that it runs exactly the opposite of what we're naturally inclined to do.

If you accept your limitations, you go beyond them.

BRENDAN BEHAN

When a dog runs at you, whistle for him.

HENRY DAVID THOREAU

If you want people to think well of you, do not speak well of yourself.

BLAISE PASCAL

For fast-acting relief, try slowing down.

LILY TOMLIN

Occasionally, a trenchant oxymoronic comment on an aspect of human behavior comes disguised in an advice-like format. An example comes from the French statesman Charles-Maurice de Talleyrand, who said nearly two centuries ago:

**Never speak ill of yourself!
You can count on your friends for that.**

Normally we think of enemies as the ones who bad-mouth us, but Talleyrand reminds us of a fascinating phenomenon—many so-called friends derive a certain pleasure from either speaking ill of us themselves or gleefully passing along the ill words of others. Mark Twain, ever alert to the perversities of human nature, put it this way:

**It takes your enemy and your friend, working together,
to hurt you to the heart; the one to slander you
and the other to get the news to you.**

Oxymoronic observations about advice-giving—especially those that capture the contradictions and ironies inherent in the process—often bring a knowing smile to people. And oxymoronic advice itself can be insightful, practical, or just plain clever, as you'll see in the remainder of this chapter.

> **I have noted that persons with bad judgment**
> **are most insistent that we do what they think best.**
>
> LIONEL ABEL

> **If you listen carefully, you get to hear everything**
> **you didn't want to hear in the first place.**
>
> SHOLEM ALEICHEM

> **What you get free costs too much.**
>
> JEAN ANOUILH

> **The surest way to lose a friend**
> **is to tell him something for his own good.**
>
> SID ASCHER

> **Never let your sense of morals get in the way of doing what's right.**
>
> ISAAC ASIMOV

> **Get it 'til it's perfect, then cut two minutes.**
>
> FRED ASTAIRE

> **If you should say, "It is enough, I have reached perfection," all is lost.**
> **For it is the function of perfection**
> **to make one know one's imperfection.**
>
> SAINT AUGUSTINE

Do you wish to rise? Begin by descending.
You plan a tower that will pierce the clouds?
Lay first the foundation of humility.

SAINT AUGUSTINE

Speak when you are angry,
and you will make the best speech you will ever regret.

AMBROSE BIERCE

Before undergoing a surgical operation, arrange your temporal affairs.
You may live.

AMBROSE BIERCE

We hate those who will not take our advice, and despise them who do.

JOSH BILLINGS (HENRY WHEELER SHAW)

Always live within your income,
even if you have to borrow money to do so.

JOSH BILLINGS

Never work before breakfast;
if you have to work before breakfast, get your breakfast first.

JOSH BILLINGS

To be believed, make the truth unbelievable.

NAPOLEON BONAPARTE

From a worldly point of view, there is no mistake so great
as that of always being right.

SAMUEL BUTLER

The highest purpose is to have no purpose at all.

JOHN CAGE

You will never live if you are looking for the meaning of life.

ALBERT CAMUS

The surest way to get a thing in this life is to be prepared
for doing without it, to the exclusion even of hope.

JANE WELSH CARLYLE

The greatest of faults . . . is to be conscious of none.

THOMAS CARLYLE

There are some occasions when a man must tell half his secret,
in order to conceal the rest.

LORD CHESTERFIELD (PHILIP DORMER STANHOPE)

Never believe anything until it has been officially denied.

CLAUD COCKBURN

Never drink black coffee at lunch;
it will keep you awake in the afternoon.

JILLY COOPER

Remember that not getting what you want
is sometimes a wonderful stroke of luck.

THE DALAI LAMA

The best thing to do with the best things in life is to give them up.

DOROTHY DAY

It is not chic to be too chic.

ELSIE DE WOLFE

If you want to be good, begin by assuming that you are bad.

EPICTETUS (FIRST CENTURY A.D.)

To seem affected, all you have to do is try to be sincere.

ANDRÉ GIDE

You can never get rid of what is part of you, even if you throw it away.

JOHANN WOLFGANG VON GOETHE

It is a great mistake to think you are more than you are
and yet to underestimate your real value.

JOHANN WOLFGANG VON GOETHE

Leave something to wish for,
so as not to be miserable from very happiness.

BALTASAR GRACIÁN

A guest should be permitted to graze, as it were,
in the pastures of his host's kindness, left even to his own devices,
like a rational being, and handsomely neglected.

LOUISE IMOGEN GUINEY

Be what you are.
This is the first step toward becoming better than you are.

J. C. HARE AND A. W. HARE

The time to relax is when you don't have time for it.

SYDNEY J. HARRIS

To be an ideal guest, stay at home.

EDGAR WATSON HOWE

The greatest mistake you can make in life
is to be continually fearing that you will make one.

ELBERT HUBBARD

When you have to make a choice and don't make it,
that is in itself a choice.

WILLIAM JAMES

Never buy what you do not want because it is cheap;
it will be dear to you.

THOMAS JEFFERSON

If you don't risk anything, you risk even more.

ERICA JONG

Don't despair, not even over the fact that you don't despair.

FRANZ KAFKA

If you are kind to people who hate themselves,
they will hate you as well.

FLORENCE KING

Thou shalt not carry moderation unto excess.

ARTHUR KOESTLER

There will come a time when you believe everything is finished.
That will be the beginning.

LOUIS L'AMOUR

The best things in life aren't things.

ANN LANDERS

Sometimes you have to be silent to be heard.

STANISLAW LEC

If a person begins by telling you,
"Do not be offended at what I am going to say,"
prepare yourself for something
that she knows will certainly offend you.

ELIZA LESLIE

Ask yourself whether you are happy, and you cease to be so.

JOHN STUART MILL

Unless we lose ourselves there is no hope of finding ourselves.

HENRY MILLER

There is only one rule for being a good talker—learn to listen.

CHRISTOPHER MORLEY

It is not good to have too much liberty.
It is not good to have all one wants.

BLAISE PASCAL

In efforts to soar above our nature we invariably fall below it.

EDGAR ALLAN POE

If you wish to forget anything on the spot,
make a note that this thing is to be remembered.

EDGAR ALLAN POE

We are so happy to advise others
that occasionally we even do it in their interest.

JULES RENARD

Be modest! It is the kind of pride least likely to offend.

JULES RENARD

Pay attention to what they tell you to forget.

MURIEL RUKEYSER

To be without some of the things you want
is an indispensable part of happiness.

BERTRAND RUSSELL

If you are lonely while you're alone, you are in bad company.

JEAN-PAUL SARTRE

Do you want to injure someone's reputation?
Don't speak ill of him, speak too well.

ANDRÉ SIEGFRIED

If you wish to preserve your secret, wrap it up in frankness.

ALEXANDER SMITH

If you want to be thought a liar, always tell the truth.

LOGAN PEARSALL SMITH

If you are too careful, you are so occupied in being careful
that you are sure to stumble over something.

GERTRUDE STEIN

Always be sincere, even if you don't mean it.

HARRY S TRUMAN

Don't play for safety. It's the most dangerous thing in the world.

HUGH WALPOLE

Stop running around after happiness.
If you make up your mind not to be happy
there's no reason why you shouldn't have a fairly good time.

EDITH WHARTON

The only way for a rich man to be healthy is,
by exercise and abstinence, to live as if he were poor.

PAUL DUDLEY WHITE

Seek simplicity and distrust it.

ALFRED NORTH WHITEHEAD

The pursuit of perfection often impedes improvement.

GEORGE WILL

A tendency to fly too straight at a goal
instead of circling around it, often carries one too far.

LIN YUTANG

chapter eleven

DESCRIPTIVE OXYMORONICA

In the popular *Prairie Home Companion* radio show, Garrison Keillor describes the fictional Minnesota town of Lake Wobegon this way:

> **Where all the women are strong,**
> **all the men are good-looking,**
> **and all the children are above average.**

Technically, it's impossible for all members of a population to be above average, so this line qualifies for entry in the paradoxical domain. Keillor's observation became a signature line for the show, and always elicits a chuckle from people who recognize it as an example of what might be called *descriptive oxymoronica*.

The best examples of descriptive oxymoronica are so tantalizing they are virtually unforgettable. These verbal gems linger on in our memories long after we first hear them. A famous Goethe observation is a good example:

Architecture is frozen music.

Yes, music flows like water. But unlike water, music cannot be frozen into ice. But what if music could be frozen? What would it look like? Goethe's description of great architecture says it all.

Oxymoronic descriptions are much more than examples of clever wordplay; they sometimes demolish conventional ways of thinking. Take a look at the dictionary definition of *sentimentality* and you will see that it is the quality of being excessively or extravagantly sentimental. No, says Norman Mailer, whose oxymoronic observation on the subject helps us see it a brand-new way:

Sentimentality is the emotional promiscuity of those who have no sentiment.

Mailer is not the only person to conclude that sentimentality is not only the absence of true sentiment, but is more accurately viewed as a counterfeit emotion masquerading as a real one:

Sentimentality, the ostentatious parading of excessive and spurious emotion, is the mark of dishonesty, the inability to feel.

JAMES BALDWIN

Sentimentality is a failure of feeling.

WALLACE STEVENS

One of the special pleasures I experienced during my research was discovering different oxymoronic descriptions of the same subject.

Notice how the following quotes all capture a paradoxical feature of that fascinating creature called *man*:

> **Man is a social animal who dislikes his fellow man.**
>
> EUGÈNE DELACROIX

> **Man is a make-believe animal—**
> **he is never so truly himself as when he is acting a part.**
>
> WILLIAM HAZLITT

> **Could anything be absurder than a man?**
> **The animal who knows everything about himself—**
> **except why he was born and the meaning of his unique life?**
>
> STORM JAMESON

> **Man is a clever animal who behaves like an imbecile.**
>
> ALBERT SCHWEITZER

> **One is tempted to define man as a rational animal**
> **who always loses his temper when he is called upon**
> **to act in accordance with the dictates of his reason.**
>
> OSCAR WILDE

Another example is *silence*. We briefly explored the concept of *sounds of silence* in an earlier chapter, but the word itself shows up nicely in some neat oxymoronic descriptions:

> **Silence. One of the hardest arguments to refute.**
>
> JOSH BILLINGS

> **Silence is more eloquent than words.**
>
> THOMAS CARLYLE

Silence is the unbearable repartee.

G. K. CHESTERTON

Silence is one of the great arts of conversation.

HANNAH MORE

And if you think that *education* is primarily an enterprise in which people learn new things on the way to becoming less ignorant, the following observations bring a fresh perspective to this centuries-old topic:

**The chief object of education is not to learn things
but to unlearn things.**

G. K. CHESTERTON

Education is a progressive discovery of our own ignorance.

WILL DURANT

**Education is what remains when we have
forgotten all that we have been taught.**

SIR GEORGE SAVILE

Education consists mainly in what we have unlearned.

MARK TWAIN

Oxymoronic descriptions sometimes begin by looking as if they're describing one thing, and unexpectedly end with a penetrating comment on something else altogether.

**Television . . . is a medium of entertainment
which permits millions of people
to listen to the same joke at the same time, and yet remain lonesome.**

T. S. ELIOT

City Life. Millions of people being lonesome together.

HENRY DAVID THOREAU

Both of these observations speak to the "quiet desperation" that, as Thoreau suggested in his famous observation, has plagued so many people in modern society. If we wanted an oxymoron to describe this pervasive phenomenon, we couldn't do much better than the expression *alone together*. The whole business has become so common that futurist Alvin Toffler wrote:

> **Loneliness is now so widespread it has become,**
> **paradoxically, a shared experience.**

Some oxymoronic descriptions simply link up contradictory or incongruous terms, like the Alec Guinness "Acting is happy agony" quote in the introduction of this book. Others involve a flat-out self-contradiction:

> **Criticism is . . . always a kind of compliment.**

JOHN MADDOX

Maddox's assertion seems nonsensical at first, but makes a good deal of sense when you stop to think about it. You see, when we become the object of criticism, it means somebody is paying attention. It means we're noteworthy enough to be criticized, which is always preferable to being ignored. Seen from this perspective, criticism is indeed a kind of compliment.

Some oxymoronic observations are so good at capturing the essence of things they may be considered *the* definitive word on the subject. Take the phenomenon of yawning. G. K. Chesterton turned his clever mind to this subject some years ago and concluded:

A yawn is a silent shout.

Not all oxymoronic descriptions are brief and pithy. Take a look at this description of tobacco from Robert Burton's 1621 book, *The Anatomy of Melancholy:*

> **Tobacco, divine, rare, superexcellent tobacco,**
> **which goes far beyond all the panaceas,**
> **potable gold, and philosophers' stones,**
> **a sovereign remedy to all diseases . . .**
> **but as it is commonly abused by most men,**
> **which take it as tinkers do ale,**
> **'tis a plague, a mischief, a violent purger of goods, lands, health;**
> **hellish, devilish and damned tobacco,**
> **the ruin and overthrow of body and soul.**

Another extended example of oxymoronica comes from the anthropologist Ruth Benedict:

> **The Japanese are, to the highest degree,**
> **both aggressive and unaggressive, both militaristic and aesthetic,**
> **both insolent and polite, rigid and adaptable,**
> **submissive and resentful of being pushed around,**
> **loyal and treacherous, brave and timid,**
> **conservative and hospitable to new ways.**

Many more examples of descriptive—and occasionally definitive—oxymoronica follow in the remainder of this chapter.

A celebrity is a person who works hard all his life to become well known, then wears dark glasses to avoid being recognized.

FRED ALLEN

Anthropology is the science which tells us that people
are the same the whole world over—except when they are different.

NANCY BANKS-SMITH

Disbelief is a form of belief.

FRANK BARRON

Nonsense is the end result of all sense.

GEORGES BATAILLE

God is the only being who, in order to reign, need not even exist.

CHARLES BAUDELAIRE

Liberty is being free from the things we don't like
in order to be slaves of the things we do like.

ERNEST BENN

Nudity is a form of dress.

JOHN BERGER

Positive, *adj.* Mistaken at the top of one's voice.

AMBROSE BIERCE

Habit, *n.* A shackle for the free.

AMBROSE BIERCE

A learned fool is one who has read everything and remembered it.

JOSH BILLINGS

Inaction may be the biggest form of action.

JERRY BROWN

Heredity is nothing but stored environment.

LUTHER BURBANK

The best memories are those we have forgotten.

ALFRED CAPUS

Violence does even justice unjustly.

THOMAS CARLYLE

Fashion is made to become unfashionable.

COCO CHANEL

Courage is almost a contradiction in terms.
It means a strong desire to live taking the form of a readiness to die.

G. K. CHESTERTON

The madman is the man who has lost everything except his reason.

G. K. CHESTERTON

There is nothing that fails like success.

G. K. CHESTERTON

War is a series of catastrophes which result in a victory.

GEORGES CLEMENCEAU

Though pride is not a virtue, it is the parent of many virtues.

JOHN CHURTON COLLINS

Paper is always strongest at the perforations.

CAROLYN M. CORRY

That's what I consider true generosity.
You give your all and yet you always feel as if it costs you nothing.

SIMONE DE BEAUVOIR

Even imperfection itself may have its ideal or perfect state.

THOMAS DE QUINCEY

Gratitude weighs heavily on us only when we no longer feel it.

COMTESSE DIANE (MARIE JOSEPHINE DE SUIN DE BEAUSACQ)

Psychology has a long past, but only a short history.

HERMANN EBBINGHAUS

Wisdom is knowing when you can't be wise.

PAUL ENGLE

The visionary is the only true realist.

FEDERICO FELLINI

None but a coward dares to boast that he has never known fear.

MARSHAL FERDINAND FOCH

Liberty is always dangerous—but it is the safest thing we have.

HARRY EMERSON FOSDICK

Of all sexual aberrations, chastity is the strangest.

ANATOLE FRANCE

Television is an invention whereby you can be entertained
in your living room by people you wouldn't have in your house.

DAVID FROST

To achieve harmony in bad taste is the height of elegance.

JEAN GENÊT

The obvious is that which is never seen
until someone expresses it simply.

KAHLIL GIBRAN

The unnatural, that too is natural.

JOHANN WOLFGANG VON GOETHE

In Utah . . . non-Mormons are theoretically subject to classification
as Gentiles, which gave rise to the well-known remark that
"Utah is the only place in the world where Jews are Gentiles."

JOHN GUNTHER

Reality is the ultimate illusion.

MAL HANCOCK

Lying is the strongest acknowledgment of the force of truth.

WILLIAM HAZLITT

Pleasure is more trouble than trouble.

DON HEROLD

Unhappiness is not knowing what we want and killing ourselves to get it.

DON HEROLD

Unpredictability, too, can become monotonous.

ERIC HOFFER

Success is ninety-nine percent failure.

SOICHIRO HONDA

Human service is the highest form of self-interest
for the person who serves.

ELBERT HUBBARD

Nonviolence is a powerful and just weapon . . .
which cuts without wounding. . . . It is a sword that heals.

MARTIN LUTHER KING JR.

It's the gossip columnist's business
to write about what is none of his business.

LOUIS KRONENBERGER

Fire is a natural symbol of life and passion,
though it is the one element in which nothing can actually live.

SUSANNE K. LANGER

A secret is what you tell someone else not to tell
because you can't keep it to yourself.

LEONARD LOUIS LEVINSON

Etiquette may be despotic,
but its cruelty is inspired by intelligent kindness.

ABBY B. LONGSTREET

Life is a tragedy full of joy.

BERNARD MALAMUD

Revenge leads to an empty fullness, like eating dirt.

MIGNON MCLAUGHLIN

Human beings are the only creatures who are able to
behave irrationally in the name of reason.

ASHLEY MONTAGU

All cities are mad; but the madness is gallant.
All cities are beautiful; but the beauty is grim.

CHRISTOPHER MORLEY

Our enemy is by tradition our savior,
in preventing us from superficiality.

JOYCE CAROL OATES

Kindness. The most unkind thing of all.

EDNA O'BRIEN

To imagine the unimaginable
is the highest use of the imagination.

CYNTHIA OZICK

Angling is an innocent cruelty.

GEORGE PARKER

A hero is a man who is afraid to run away.

PROVERB (ENGLISH)

Dignity is the quality that enables a man who
says nothing, does nothing, and knows nothing
to command a great deal of respect.

JOHN W. RAPER

Passion makes the best observations
and draws the most wretched conclusions.

JEAN PAUL RICHTER

Inspiration could be called
inhaling the memory of an act never experienced.

NED ROREM

There is a degree of tolerance which borders on insult.

JEAN ROSTAND

Freedom is the right to choose the habits that bind you.

RENATE RUBENSTEIN

Work is man's most natural form of relaxation.

DAGOBERT RUNES

Sanity is madness put to good uses.

GEORGE SANTAYANA

Curiosity is one of those insatiable passions that grow by gratification.

SARAH SCOTT

Suicide . . . is about life,
being in fact the sincerest form of criticism life gets.

WILFRID SHEED

Quite literally, a man's memory is what he forgets with.

ODELL SHEPARD

Camp asserts . . . there is a good taste of bad taste.

SUSAN SONTAG

Sanity is a cozy lie.

SUSAN SONTAG

Giving is true having.

CHARLES HADDON SPURGEON

Realism is a corruption of reality.

WALLACE STEVENS

Statistics are but mendacious truths.

LIONEL STRACHEY

Vision is the art of seeing things invisible.

JONATHAN SWIFT

Civilization is a limitless multiplication of unnecessary necessaries.

MARK TWAIN

That weakness in human nature which goes by the name of strength.

PETER USTINOV

Servitude debases men to the point where they end up liking it.

MARQUIS DE VAUVENARGUES (LUC DE CLAPIERS)

Common sense is not so common.

VOLTAIRE

What is madness? To have erroneous perceptions
and to reason correctly from them.

VOLTAIRE

Basic research is when I'm doing what I don't know I'm doing.

WERNHER VON BRAUN

Fire destroys that which feeds it.

SIMONE WEIL

Purity is the ability to contemplate defilement.

SIMONE WEIL

War is fear cloaked in courage.

WILLIAM C. WESTMORELAND

Liberty is the only thing you cannot have
unless you are willing to give it to others.

WILLIAM ALLEN WHITE

A cigarette is the perfect type of perfect pleasure.
It is exquisite and it leaves one unsatisfied.

OSCAR WILDE

chapter twelve

THE LITERARY LIFE

In his 1922 rectorial address at St. Andrews University in Scotland, the noted English playwright J. M. Barrie said of writers:

> **We are all failures—at least, all the best of us are.**

Barrie's point, if I interpret him correctly, is that writing at a high level is so difficult that even great writers rarely consider themselves truly successful at it. It's an ancient oxymoronic theme that applies to other disciplines as well. It was first noted by Confucius twenty-five hundred years ago:

> **The superior man is distressed by his lack of ability.**

Many talented writers and poets have made this same point over the years, some seriously and some with great wit:

It took me fifteen years to discover that I had no talent for writing,
but I couldn't give it up because by that time I was too famous.

ROBERT C. BENCHLEY

I don't think I am any good. If I thought I was any good, I wouldn't be.

JOHN BETJEMAN

By the time a writer discovers he has no talent for literature,
he is too successful to give it up.

GEORGE S. KAUFMAN

When the best practitioners of an enterprise consider themselves failures at it, the activity they are describing must be difficult. And, in an ironic twist, the better a writer one is, the more difficult writing seems:

A writer is somebody for whom writing is
more difficult than it is for other people.

THOMAS MANN

Writing came easy—it would only get hard when I got better at it.

GARY WILLS

Of course, writing doesn't seem so difficult from the perspective of many readers, who often look at a book the way museum visitors look at a painting, and think: "I could do that." Noticing this phenomenon, William Hazlitt observed:

The only impeccable writers are those that never wrote.

Indeed, writing is so challenging that many talented writers have resorted to humor to describe the difficulty—and sometimes the terror—they experience when sitting in front of a typewriter or key-board and trying to bring life to thoughts and ideas that never before existed in print.

> **Writing is easy; all you do is sit staring at a blank sheet of paper until the drops of blood form on your forehead.**
>
> GENE FOWLER

> **Contrary to what many of you might imagine, a career in letters is not without its drawbacks— chief among them the unpleasant fact that one is frequently called upon to sit down and write.**
>
> FRAN LEBOWITZ

Another problem confronting writers is the task of editing their own creations. In yet another fascinating wrinkle, many people have noted that what seem to be the finest creations often turn out to be a writer's worst. Dr. Samuel Johnson quoted one of his college tutors as having imparted this great writing advice:

> **Read over your compositions, and whenever you meet with a passage which you think is particularly fine, strike it out.**

Because writers—like all people—have a capacity for self-deception, it's difficult for them to judge the quality of their own creations. Others in the literary world have noticed this problem, and suggested a similar remedy:

> **Every writer hits now and then upon a thought that seems to him so happy,**

> a repartee that amuses him so much,
> that to cut it is worse than having a tooth out;
> it is then that it is well to have engraved on his heart the maxim,
> If you can, cut.
>
> W. SOMERSET MAUGHAM

> If you require a practical rule of me, I will present you with this:
> Whenever you feel an impulse to perpetrate
> a piece of exceptionally fine writing, obey it—whole-heartedly—
> and delete it before sending your manuscript to press.
> *Murder your darlings.*
>
> SIR ARTHUR QUILLER-COUCH

The things that writers choose to write about have also been described in memorable oxymoronic fashion. In his poem "Bishop Blougram's Apology," Robert Browning described the motivation of many a writer:

> Our interest's on the dangerous edge of things.
> The honest thief, the tender murderer,
> The superstitious atheist.

What Browning is suggesting, I believe, is that writers are drawn to the complex and contradictory aspects of life. The English writer Graham Greene was so taken with this passage—and so convinced that it captured the things he was most interested in writing about—that he said it could serve as the epigraph for every one of his novels.

No excursion into oxymoronic observations about the literary life would be complete without mentioning the people to whom books are dedicated. The typical dedication is usually a sweet—and occasionally sappy—note of appreciation to a loved one, often someone who's been neglected during the long and arduous process of producing the book. But what if an author set his or her mind to composing a wickedly clever—and deliciously oxymoronic—dedication? P. G. Wodehouse did exactly that in the dedication to his 1926 book, *Heart of a Goof*:

> **To my daughter Leonora**
> **without whose never-failing sympathy and encouragement**
> **this book would have been finished in half the time.**

Over the centuries, writers have made numerous oxymoronic observations about the literary life. If you're a writer, or simply someone who appreciates great writing, I think you'll enjoy these observations.

> **The best part of the fiction in many novels**
> **is the notice that the characters are purely imaginary.**
>
> FRANKLIN P. ADAMS

> **Having imagination, it takes you an hour to write a paragraph that,**
> **if you were unimaginative, would take you only a minute.**
> **Or you might not write the paragraph at all.**
>
> FRANKLIN P. ADAMS

> **It is the business of the tragic poet to give audiences**
> **the pleasure which arises from pity and terror.**
>
> ARISTOTLE (FOURTH CENTURY B.C.)

> **The most corrected copies are commonly the least correct.**
>
> FRANCIS BACON

The things which matter most
are readily understood and easy to describe,
but when it comes to the minor affairs of life
one has to go into a great deal of detail.

HONORÉ DE BALZAC

Only those ideas that are least truly ours
can be adequately expressed in words.

HENRI BERGSON

It is one of the paradoxes of American literature
that our writers are forever looking back with love and nostalgia
at lives they couldn't wait to leave.

ANATOLE BROYARD

To finish is both a relief and a release
from an extraordinarily pleasant prison.

ROBERT BURCHFIELD, ON COMPLETING
THE *OXFORD ENGLISH DICTIONARY*

I write of melancholy, by being busy to avoid melancholy.

ROBERT BURTON

I write of the wish that comes true—
for some reason, a terrifying concept.

JAMES M. CAIN

I got this idea of doing a really serious big work—
it would be precisely like a novel, with a single difference:
every word of it would be true from beginning to end.

TRUMAN CAPOTE, ON *IN COLD BLOOD* (1966),
WHICH HE CALLED "A NONFICTION NOVEL"

The man is most original who
can adapt from the greatest number of sources.

THOMAS CARLYLE

You could compile the worst book in the world entirely out of
selected passages from the best writers in the world.

G. K. CHESTERTON

Poetry lies its way to the truth.

JOHN CIARDI

You explain nothing, O poet,
but thanks to you all things become explicable.

PAUL CLAUDEL

The poet is a liar who always speaks the truth.

JEAN COCTEAU

The faults of great authors are
generally excellences carried to an excess.

SAMUEL TAYLOR COLERIDGE

There is a pleasure in poetic pains
Which only poets know.

WILLIAM COWPER

I love being a writer. What I hate is the paperwork.

PETER DE VRIES

If there is one major cause for the spread of mass illiteracy,
it's the fact that everybody can read and write.

PETER DE VRIES

The business of the poet is not to find new emotions,
but to use the ordinary ones and, in working them up into poetry,
to express feelings which are not in actual emotions at all.

T. S. ELIOT

Good fiction is made of that which is real.

RALPH ELLISON

The book written against fame and learning
has the author's name on the title page.

RALPH WALDO EMERSON

If you want to be true to life, start lying about it.

JOHN FOWLES

All the good writers of confessions, from Augustine onwards,
are men who are still a little in love with their sins.

ANATOLE FRANCE

If a young writer can refrain from writing,
he shouldn't hesitate to do so.

ANDRÉ GIDE

It is with noble sentiments that bad literature gets written.

ANDRÉ GIDE

Journalism will kill you, but it will keep you alive while you're at it.

HORACE GREELEY

If I gave up teaching, I would have no time at all for writing.

JOSEPH HELLER

While none of the work we do is very important,
it is important that we do a great deal of it.

JOSEPH HELLER

All good books are alike in that
they are truer than if they had really happened.

ERNEST HEMINGWAY

To write a quality cliché you have to come up with something new.

JENNY HOLZER

What is called a sincere work is one that is
endowed with enough strength to give reality to an illusion.

MAX JACOB

The artist is present in every page of every book
from which he sought so assiduously to eliminate himself.

HENRY JAMES

We make up horrors to help us cope with the real ones.

STEPHEN KING

Write a nonfiction book, and be prepared
for the legion of readers who are going to doubt your facts.
But write a novel, and get ready
for the world to assume every word is true.

BARBARA KINGSOLVER

A journalist is stimulated by a deadline;
he writes worse when he has time.

KARL KRAUS

The novelist says in words what cannot be said in words.

URSULA K. LE GUIN

If it sounds like writing, I rewrite it.

ELMORE LEONARD

A biographer is an artist who is on oath,
and anyone who knows anything about artists,
knows that that is almost a contradiction in terms.

DESMOND MACCARTHY

A literary movement consists of five or six people who
live in the same town and hate each other cordially.

GEORGE MOORE

It takes less time to learn how to write nobly
than how to write lightly and straightforwardly.

FRIEDRICH NIETZSCHE

Writing biography is a paradoxical enterprise,
at once solitary and communal.

PENELOPE NIVEN

Everywhere I go, I'm asked if I think the universities stifle writers.
My opinion is that they don't stifle enough of them.
There's many a best-seller that
could have been prevented by a good teacher.

FLANNERY O'CONNOR

The existence of good bad literature—
the fact that one can be amused or excited or even moved by a book

that one's intellect simply refuses to take seriously—
is a reminder that art is not the same thing as celebration.

GEORGE ORWELL, IN THE ESSAY "GOOD BAD BOOKS" (1950)

Even those who write against fame
wish for the fame of having written well.

BLAISE PASCAL

Misquotations are the only quotations that are never misquoted.

HESKETH PEARSON

A good novel is possible only after one has given up and let go.

WALKER PERCY

Literature: proclaiming in front of everyone
what one is careful to conceal from one's immediate circle.

JEAN ROSTAND

Many learned persons have read themselves stupid.

ARTHUR SCHOPENHAUER

The lesson intended by an author is hardly ever
the lesson the world chooses to learn from his book.

GEORGE BERNARD SHAW

I claim to be a conscientiously immoral writer.

GEORGE BERNARD SHAW

The man who writes about himself and his own time
is the only man who writes about all people and about all time.

GEORGE BERNARD SHAW

I never read a book before reviewing it; it prejudices one so.

SYDNEY SMITH

A good writer always works at the impossible.

JOHN STEINBECK

A successful book is not made of what is in it, but what is left out of it.

MARK TWAIN

It takes a heap of sense to write good nonsense.

MARK TWAIN

There's always something new
by looking at the same thing over and over.

JOHN UPDIKE

In poetry, everything which must be said
is almost impossible to say well.

PAUL VALÉRY

Originality is nothing but judicious imitation.

VOLTAIRE

There is so much nastiness in modern literature
that I like to write stories which contain
nothing more than a little innocent murdering.

EDGAR WALLACE

Fiction reveals truths that reality obscures.

JESSAMYN WEST

Be obscure clearly.

E. B. WHITE

Damn all expurgated books;
the dirtiest book of all is the expurgated book.

WALT WHITMAN

It is much easier to write a long book than a short one.

I. M. WISE (ISAAC MEYER)

chapter thirteen

OXYMORONIC INSIGHTS FROM
WORLD LITERATURE

George Orwell's classic *Animal Farm* contains these familiar words:

All animals are equal,
but some animals are more equal than others.

In *Les Misérables,* Victor Hugo penned a line that is equally provocative, if not as well known:

The malicious have a dark happiness.

And Charles Dickens opens *A Tale of Two Cities* with an oxymoronic tour de force:

It was the best of times, it was the worst of times,
it was the age of wisdom, it was the age of foolishness,
it was the epoch of belief, it was the epoch of incredulity,
it was the season of Light, it was the season of Darkness,
it was the spring of hope, it was the winter of despair,
we had everything before us, we had nothing before us,
we were all going direct to Heaven,
we were all going direct the other way.

When writers use oxymoronic phrasing, their goal is not simply to demonstrate verbal virtuosity (although that is clearly part of the motivation); it is also to compel the attention of readers and help them deepen their understanding of life's intriguing realities. Another classic example comes from *The Canterbury Tales*, when Geoffrey Chaucer wrote (in Old English style):

Poverte is hateful good.

Chaucer's point has been made many times over the centuries—even though people growing up in poverty are often unhappy with their lot in life, there are benefits that come from being raised in dire circumstances. This notion shows up in the comments of many successful people as they reflect on their lives. Here are two examples from the modern world of show business:

My children didn't have my advantages:
I was born into abject poverty.

KIRK DOUGLAS

**The two big advantages I had at birth
were to have been born wise
and to have been born in poverty.**

SOPHIA LOREN

In his fifteenth-century classic tale, *Le Morte d'Arthur*, Sir Thomas
Malory wrote about King Arthur:

**And many men say
there is written upon his tomb this verse:
"Here lies Arthur, the once and future king."**

One cannot be both a past and a future king, so the expression is
clearly self-contradictory. What does this legendary line mean? It may
have reflected the common belief at the time that Arthur was not
really dead and would one day return to win the Holy Grail. Or
maybe, like Jesus, he would rise from the dead and return to the
throne. It might even have meant that Arthur was without peer and
would forever be known as England's greatest king. Whatever the
precise meaning, it's a neat bit of oxymoronic phrasing, and one that
has thrilled many a reader over the centuries.

In addition to telling a good story, the goal of every writer is to
compose memorable and compelling lines. And no writer has
composed as many as William Shakespeare. We've seen many
oxymoronic creations from the Bard in other chapters; here are a few
more famous examples:

I do desire we may be better strangers.

AS YOU LIKE IT

**I must be cruel
only to be kind.**

HAMLET

Striving to better, oft we mar what's well.

KING LEAR

Parting is such sweet sorrow.

ROMEO AND JULIET

**You pay a great deal too dear
for what's given freely.**

THE WINTER'S TALE

Remarkable examples of oxymoronica appear in the works of great writers from every country and every literary genre. In Jane Austen's *Pride and Prejudice*, Mr. Bennett happily listens to his daughter Mary sing, but eventually tires of the experience. In a line all parents of young children can appreciate, he finally says:

You have delighted us long enough.

Many of Austen's descriptions of the ordinary experiences of people are priceless examples of oxymoronica:

**Elinor agreed with it all, for she did not think
he deserved the compliment of rational opposition.**

SENSE AND SENSIBILITY (1811)

**Mrs. Long is a selfish, hypocritical woman,
and I have no opinion of her.**

PRIDE AND PREJUDICE (1813)

It was a delightful visit—perfect, in being much too short.

EMMA (1815)

I cannot speak well enough to be unintelligible.

NORTHANGER ABBEY (1818)

Austen was so fond of paradoxical phrasing that she even used it in her correspondence. In a 1798 letter to her sister Cassandra, written when she was only twenty-three, she wrote:

I do not want people to be very agreeable,
as it saves me the trouble of liking them a great deal.

The trouble of liking people? Her disclosure captures the ambivalence that shy people—and occasionally even extroverts—feel about social interaction. Even time spent with likeable and enjoyable people can sometimes come at a cost.

In *Notes from the Underground*, first published in 1864, the great Russian writer Fyodor Dostoyevsky offered two remarkable glimpses into the human soul:

In despair there are the most intense enjoyments,
especially when one is very acutely conscious
of the hopelessness of one's position.

Man is sometimes extraordinarily,
passionately, in love with suffering.

Other penetrating thinkers have also noticed this somewhat puzzling, but very human phenomenon. In *Beyond Good and Evil* (1885), Friedrich Nietzsche wrote:

The thought of suicide is a great consolation:
with the help of it one has got through many a bad night.

Thinking along the same lines, the French playwright Jean Anouilh noted:

> **You may not know it, but at the far end of despair,**
> **there is a white clearing where one is almost happy.**

Notice how the same theme gets played out in three other novels:

> **Despair itself, if it goes on long enough, can become**
> **a kind of sanctuary in which one settles down and feels at ease.**
> CHARLES-AUGUSTIN SAINTE-BEUVE, IN
> *THE LIFE OF JOSEPH DELORME* (1829)

> **There is a stage in any misery when**
> **the victim begins to find a deep satisfaction in it.**
> STORM JAMESON, IN *THAT WAS YESTERDAY* (1932)

> **At times it is strangely sedative**
> **to know the extent of your own powerlessness.**
> ERICA JONG, IN *FEAR OF FLYING* (1973)

Because a writer looks at human beings through the eyes of an artist and a detached observer, important psychological insights are just as likely—maybe even more likely—to be described in works of fiction, rather than in psychology texts. In her first novel, *The Bluest Eye* (1970), Toni Morrison put her finger on something that has perplexed and frustrated distraught people for decades—the unhelpfulness of so many practitioners in the helping professions:

> **As in the case of many misanthropes, his disdain for people**
> **led him into a profession designed to serve them.**

Whether they come from luminaries in literary history or writers who are not particularly well known, oxymoronic literary passages reveal essential truths about the human experience, as you will continue to see in the remainder of this chapter.

Once again she decided not to decide.
She preferred being compelled into her decisions.

LISA ALTHER, IN *KINFLICKS* (1975)

Show me one who boasts continually of his "openness,"
and I will show you one who conceals much.

MINNA THOMAS ANTRIM, IN
AT THE SIGN OF THE GOLDEN CALF (1905)

There is a politeness so terrible, that rage beside it is balm.

MINNA THOMAS ANTRIM, IN
AT THE SIGN OF THE GOLDEN CALF (1905)

The unendurable is the beginning of the curve of joy.

DJUNA BARNES, IN *NIGHTWOOD* (1937)

Nothing is funnier than unhappiness.

SAMUEL BECKETT, IN *ENDGAME* (1958)

Birth was the death of him.

SAMUEL BECKETT, IN *A PIECE OF MONOLOGUE* (1979)

Entertaining is one method of avoiding people.

ELIZABETH BIBESCO, IN *THE FIR AND THE PALM* (1924)

The innocent are so few that two of them seldom meet—
when they do meet, their victims lie strewn all round.

ELIZABETH BOWEN, IN *THE DEATH OF THE HEART* (1938)

I've noticed your hostility to him . . .
I ought to have guessed you were friends.

MALCOLM BRADBURY, IN *THE HISTORY MAN* (1970)

How does a man live? By completely forgetting he is a human being.

BERTOLT BRECHT, IN *THE THREEPENNY OPERA* (1928)

Because I don't trust him, we are friends.

BERTOLT BRECHT, IN *MOTHER COURAGE* (1939)

The rule is, jam tomorrow and jam yesterday—but never jam today.

LEWIS CARROLL, IN *THROUGH THE LOOKING-GLASS* (1872)

There is no robbery so terrible as the robbery committed
by those who think they are doing right.

MARY CATHERWOOD, IN *LAZARRE* (1901)

What is bought is cheaper than a gift.

MIGUEL DE CERVANTES, IN *DON QUIXOTE* (1605)

Promise is most given when the least is said.

GEORGE CHAPMAN, IN *HERO AND LEANDER* (1598)

The handsome gifts that fate and nature lend us
most often are the very ones that end us.

GEOFFREY CHAUCER, IN *THE CANTERBURY TALES* (C.1387–1400)

The latter end of joy is woe.
GEOFFREY CHAUCER, IN *THE CANTERBURY TALES* (C.1387–1400)

**When a lot of remedies are suggested for a disease,
that means it can't be cured.**
ANTON CHEKHOV, IN *THE CHERRY ORCHARD* (1904)

It is completely unimportant. That is why it is so interesting.
AGATHA CHRISTIE, IN *THE MURDER OF ROGER ACKROYD* (1926)

**Too much mercy . . . often resulted in further crimes which were
fatal to innocent victims who need not have been victims
if justice had been put first and mercy second.**
AGATHA CHRISTIE, IN *THE HALLOWEEN PARTY* (1969)

A man's most open actions have been a secret side to them.
JOSEPH CONRAD, IN *UNDER WESTERN EYES* (1911)

My dearest hope is to lose all hope.
PIERRE CORNEILLE, IN *LE CID* (1636)

**Everybody was up to something, especially, of course,
those who were up to nothing.**
NOEL COWARD, IN *FUTURE INDEFINITE* (1954)

Leaving can sometimes be the best way to never go away.
CATHY N. DAVIDSON, IN *36 VIEWS OF MOUNT FUJI* (1993)

**It is the final proof of God's omnipotence
that he need not exist in order to save us.**
PETER DE VRIES, IN *MACKEREL PLAZA* (1958)

He is an honorable, obstinate, truthful, high-spirited,
intensely prejudiced, perfectly reasonable man.

CHARLES DICKENS, IN *BLEAK HOUSE* (1852)

There is moderation even in excess.

BENJAMIN DISRAELI, IN *VIVIAN GRAY* (1826)

"Frank and explicit"—that is the right line to take
when you wish to conceal your own mind and
to confuse the minds of others.

BENJAMIN DISRAELI, IN *SYBIL* (1845)

Depend upon it, there is nothing so unnatural as the commonplace.

ARTHUR CONAN DOYLE, IN "A CASE OF IDENTITY" (1891)

The only truth lies in learning to free ourselves
from insane passion for the truth.

UMBERTO ECO, IN *THE NAME OF THE ROSE* (1980)

One way of getting an idea of our fellow-countrymen's miseries
is to go and look at their pleasures.

GEORGE ELIOT, IN *THE RADICAL* (1866)

The desire to conquer is itself a sort of subjection.

GEORGE ELIOT, IN *DANIEL DERONDA* (1876)

No evil dooms us hopelessly except the evil we love,
and desire to continue in, and make no effort to escape from.

GEORGE ELIOT, IN *DANIEL DERONDA* (1876)

The practice of deception was so constant with her
that it got to be a kind of truth.

LOUISE ERDRICH, IN *TRACKS* (1988)

Part of getting over it is knowing that you will never get over it.

ANNE FINGER, IN *PAST DUE* (1990)

Those who have given themselves the most concern about
the happiness of people have made their neighbors very miserable.

ANATOLE FRANCE, IN
THE CRIME OF SYLVESTRE BONNARD (1881)

Most people work the greater part of their time for a mere living;
and the little freedom which remains to them so troubles them
that they use every means of getting rid of it.

JOHANN WOLFGANG VON GOETHE, IN
THE SORROWS OF YOUNG WERTHER (1774)

If I love you, what business is it of yours?

JOHANN WOLFGANG VON GOETHE, IN
WILHELM MEISTER'S APPRENTICESHIP (1786)

She saw now that the strong impulses
which had once wrecked her happiness
were the forces that had enabled her
to rebuild her life out of the ruins.

ELLEN GLASGOW, IN *BARREN GROUND* (1925)

There are some faults so nearly allied to excellence,
that we can scarcely weed out the fault
without eradicating the virtue.

OLIVER GOLDSMITH, IN *THE GOOD-NATUR'D MAN* (1768)

My mother and father and I now lived in the intimacy of estrangement
that exists between married couples who
have nothing left in common but their incompatibility.

NADINE GORDIMER, IN *THE LYING DAYS* (1953)

That man's silence is wonderful to listen to.

THOMAS HARDY, IN *UNDER THE GREENWOOD TREE* (1872)

Anything free costs twice as much
in the long run or turns out worthless.

ROBERT A. HEINLEIN, IN
THE MOON IS A HARSH MISTRESS (1966)

Even amongst men lacking all distinction he inevitably stood out
as a man lacking more distinction than all the rest,
and people who met him were always impressed
by how unimpressive he was.

JOSEPH HELLER, IN *CATCH-22* (1961)

The Texan turned out to be good-natured, generous and likable.
In three days no one could stand him.

JOSEPH HELLER, IN *CATCH-22* (1961)

There was only one catch and that was Catch-22,
which specified that a concern for one's own safety
in the face of dangers that were real and immediate
was the process of a rational mind.
If Orr flew more combat missions, he was crazy and didn't have to;
but if he didn't want to he was sane and had to.

JOSEPH HELLER, IN *CATCH-22* (1961)

When I grow up I want to be a little boy.

JOSEPH HELLER, IN *SOMETHING HAPPENED* (1974)

No yellow armband, no marked park bench, no Gestapo.
Just here a flick and there another . . .
But day by day the little thump of insult.
Day by day the tapping on the nerves,
the delicate assault on the proud stuff of a man's identity.

LAURA HOBSON, IN *GENTLEMAN'S AGREEMENT* (1947)

You have no idea, sir,
how difficult it is to be the victim of benevolence.

JANE AIKEN HODGE, IN *MARRY IN HASTE* (1961)

He had felt like a man rushing to catch a train
he was anxious to miss.

HELEN HUDSON, IN *MEYER MEYER* (1967)

That is the way with people . . . If they do you wrong,
they invent a bad name for you, a good name for their acts,
and then destroy you in the name of virtue.

ZORA NEALE HURSTON, IN
MOSES: MAN OF THE MOUNTAIN (1939)

Several excuses are always less convincing than one.

ALDOUS HUXLEY, IN *POINT COUNTER POINT* (1928)

Whenever a man's friends begin to
compliment him about looking young,
he may be sure that they think he is growing old.

WASHINGTON IRVING, IN *BRACEBRIDGE HALL* (1822)

The unforgivable was usually the most easily forgiven.

P. D. JAMES, IN *DEATH OF AN EXPERT WITNESS* (1977)

I shall long to see the miseries of the world,
since the sight of them is necessary to happiness.

DR. SAMUEL JOHNSON, IN *RASSELAS* (1759)

Nobody gets packed off to the insane asylum in Our Town.
Dotty people are just accepted, and everybody watches them
and takes care of them because everybody knows
the ones who really need watching
are the people who are supposed to be all right.

CAROLYN KENMORE, IN *MANNEQUIN* (1969)

But it's the truth even if it didn't happen.

KEN KESEY, IN *ONE FLEW OVER THE CUCKOO'S NEST* (1962)

A meaningless phrase repeated again and again
begins to resemble truth.

BARBARA KINGSOLVER, IN *ANIMAL DREAMS* (1990)

Maybe selflessness was only selfishness on another level.

MARGARET LANDON, IN *ANNA AND THE KING OF SIAM* (1944)

To oppose something is to maintain it.

URSULA K. LE GUIN, IN *THE LEFT HAND OF DARKNESS* (1969)

He had grown up in a country run by politicians
who sent the pilots to man the bombers to kill the babies
to make the world safe for children to grow up in.

URSULA K. LE GUIN, IN *THE LATHE OF HEAVEN* (1971)

He knew that in so far as one denies what is,
one is possessed by what is not,
the compulsions, the fantasies, the terrors that flock to fill the void.

URSULA K. LE GUIN, IN *THE LATHE OF HEAVEN* (1971)

When a white man in Africa by accident
looks into the eyes of a native and sees the human being
(which it is his chief preoccupation to avoid),
his sense of guilt, which he denies, fumes up in resentment
and he brings down the whip.

DORIS LESSING, IN *THE GRASS IS SINGING* (1950)

Too much freedom is its own kind of cage.

PATRICIA MACDONALD, IN *SECRET ADMIRER* (1995)

Just remember enough never to be vulnerable again:
total forgetting could be as self-destructive
as complete remembering.

HELEN MACINNES, IN *THE VENETIAN AFFAIR* (1963)

We are most likely to get angry and excited
in our opposition to some idea
when we ourselves are not quite certain of our own position,
and are inwardly tempted to take the other side.

THOMAS MANN, IN *BUDDENBROOKS* (1903)

Solitude gives birth to the original in us,
to beauty unfamiliar and perilous—to poetry.
But also it gives birth to the opposite:
to the perverse, the illicit, the absurd.

THOMAS MANN, IN *DEATH IN VENICE* (1913)

I would be content being a housewife if I could find
the kind of man who wouldn't treat me like one.

TERRY MCMILLAN, IN *WAITING TO EXHALE* (1992)

There are some enterprises in which
a careful disorderliness is the true method.

HERMAN MELVILLE, IN *MOBY-DICK* (1851)

War is peace. Freedom is slavery. Ignorance is strength.

GEORGE ORWELL, IN *1984* (1948)

The best place to hide anything is in plain view.

EDGAR ALLAN POE, IN *THE PURLOINED LETTER* (1844)

Every major horror of history was committed
in the name of an altruistic motive.
Has any act of selfishness ever equaled the carnage
perpetrated by disciples of altruism?

AYN RAND, IN *THE FOUNTAINHEAD* (1943)

A mark was on him from the day's delight, so that all his life,
when April was a thin green and the flavor of rain was on his tongue,
an old wound would throb and a nostalgia would fill him
for something he could not quite remember.

MARJORIE KINNAN RAWLINGS, IN *THE YEARLING* (1938)

"Certainly." He beamed uncertainly. "Certainly."

HOLLY ROTH, IN *BUTTON, BUTTON* (1966)

Patience is bitter, but its fruit is sweet.

JEAN JACQUES ROUSSEAU, IN *ÉMILE* (1762)

I think she must have been very strictly brought up,
she's so desperately anxious to do the wrong thing correctly.

SAKI (H. H. MUNRO), IN "REGINALD ON WORRIES" (1904)

You can't expect a boy to be vicious till he's been to a good school.
SAKI (H. H. MUNRO), IN "THE BAKER'S DOZEN" (1910)

I'm quite illiterate, but I read a lot.
J. D. SALINGER, IN *THE CATCHER IN THE RYE* (1951)

Forgiveness is the one unpardonable sin.
DOROTHY L. SAYERS, IN *THE FIVE RED HERRINGS* (1931)

There is nothing more tedious than a constant round of gaiety.
MARGERY SHARP, IN *THE RESCUERS* (1959)

The most unbearable pain is produced
by prolonging the keenest pleasure.
GEORGE BERNARD SHAW, IN *MAN AND SUPERMAN* (1903)

The surest way to ruin a man who doesn't
know how to handle money is to give him some.
GEORGE BERNARD SHAW, IN *HEARTBREAK HOUSE* (1919)

You only have power over people as long as you don't take
everything away from them. But when you've robbed
a man of *everything* he's no longer in your power—he's free again.
ALEXANDER SOLZHENITSYN, IN *THE FIRST CIRCLE* (1968)

Oh, I wish that God had not given me what I prayed for!
It was not so good as I thought.
JOHANNA SPYRI, IN *HEIDI* (1880)

Oh, isn't life a terrible thing, thank God?
DYLAN THOMAS, IN *UNDER MILK WOOD* (1954)

I know I am among civilized men because
they are fighting so savagely.

VOLTAIRE, IN *CANDIDE* (1758)

Individual misfortunes give rise to the general good;
so that the more individual misfortunes exist, the more all is fine.

VOLTAIRE, IN *CANDIDE* (1758)

She usually liked everybody most when they weren't there.

ELIZABETH VON ARNIM, IN *THE ENCHANTED APRIL* (1922)

People do not wish to appear foolish; to avoid the appearance
of foolishness, they were willing actually to remain fools.

ALICE WALKER, IN
IN SEARCH OF OUR MOTHERS' GARDENS (1979)

The only way not to think about money is to have a great deal of it.

EDITH WHARTON, IN *THE HOUSE OF MIRTH* (1905)

Some things are best mended by a break.

EDITH WHARTON, IN *THE CUSTOM OF THE COUNTRY* (1913)

The door behind him opened, and Beach the butler entered,
a dignified procession of one.

P. G. WODEHOUSE, IN *LEAVE IT TO PSMITH* (1923)

Maybe love can kill better than hate.

MAIA WOJCIECHOWSKA, IN *A SINGLE LIGHT* (1968)

chapter fourteen

INADVERTENT OXYMORONICA

S ome of the most interesting oxymoronic observations come
about by accident. Many are an integral part of popular culture:

I can give you a definite perhaps.

SAMUEL GOLDWYN

**If people don't want to come out to the ball park,
nobody's going to stop them.**

YOGI BERRA

Prominent public figures are a great source of what might be called
inadvertent oxymoronica. A few years back, Sylvester Stallone said of
himself:

I'm the Hiroshima of love.

Not to be outclassed, fellow actor John Travolta said to an interviewer:

If I'm androgynous, I'd say I lean towards macho-androgynous.

Actors aren't the only public figures capable of such remarks. Rock stars have offered many memorable examples:

I'm not a snob. Ask anybody. Well, anybody who matters.
SIMON LEBON, OF DURAN DURAN

**The only luxury is freedom . . . They can chop off my head
and take everything else as long as they leave me that.**
DIETER MEIER, OF THE ROCK GROUP YELLO

**It's really hard to maintain a one-on-one relationship
if the other person is not going to allow me to be with other people.**
AXL ROSE, OF GUNS 'N' ROSES

Professional athletes have also contributed some wonderful examples:

We have only one person to blame, and that's each other.
BARRY BACK, AFTER A NEW YORK RANGERS LOSS

**We all played poorly. It wasn't just one guy's fault.
It was a real team effort.**
ARNETTE HALLMAN, AFTER A TEAM LOSS

Humility is something I've always prided myself on.
BERNIE KOSAR, NFL QUARTERBACK

I want to gain 1,500 or 2,000 yards, whichever comes first.

GEORGE ROGERS, ON HIS NFL GOALS

It's about 90% strength and 40% technique.

JOHNNY WALKER, ON SUCCESSFUL WRIST-WRESTLING

Examples of inadvertent oxymoronica show up in the most unexpected places. In his 1970 book *The Cutting Edge*, Louis Kronenberger described an Irish gravestone that contained a remarkable epitaph:

**Erected to the Memory of
John Phillips
Accidentally Shot
As a Mark of Affection by his Brother**

Another emerged in the 2001 trial of rap star Sean "Puffy" Combs (aka "Puff Daddy" and "P. Diddy") for possession of illegal firearms and attempting to bribe a witness. In opening remarks to the jury, defense attorney Benjamin Brafman said:

**Mr. Combs does not want an advantage because he is a superstar.
But he is not entitled to a disadvantage, either.**

Church bulletins are also a great source of inadvertent oxymoronica. Thanks to the ability to "forward" e-mails, misstatements found in church bulletins are quickly shared with friends and family—and then the rest of the world. Here are a few gems I've discovered in my research:

**The cost for attending the Fasting and Prayer Conference
includes meals.**

**The peacemaking meeting scheduled for today
has been canceled due to a conflict.**

**Irving Benson and Jessie Carter were married
on October 24 in the church.
So ends a friendship that began in their school days.**

For many years, inadvertent oxymoronic observations have often
gone by the name "bulls" (or "Irish Bulls"). The *Oxford English Dictionary* defines *bull* this way:

> *A self-contradictory proposition; in modern use, an
> expression containing a manifest contradiction in
> terms or involving a ludicrous inconsistency unperceived by the speaker. Now often (used) with the epithet Irish; but the word had been long in use before it
> came to be associated with Irishmen.*

As the definition makes clear, there's nothing particularly Irish about
bulls. But sometime in the distant past, English snobs appropriated the
term to express their disdain for the Irish. Unfortunately, it stuck.
Ever since, the expression has been used to tell a highly specific type of
ethnic joke—one in which Irish people are unaware of the illogical or
ridiculous nature of their remarks. A classic is the one about the Irish
drunk in a Dublin court who says in his defense:

Yur hahnner, I was sober enough to know I was dhroonk.

In truth, there was a real Irish politician who was famous for these
kinds of remarks, a fact that probably helped popularize the concept of
an Irish Bull. Sir Boyle Roche was one of the most colorful politicians
of the eighteenth century, for many years serving as an Irish member

of the British Parliament. Long before the world ever heard of Samuel Goldwyn or Yogi Berra, people in Roche's time were fascinated by his misadventures with the English language. During a heated parliamentary debate, he once replied:

I answer in the affirmative with an emphatic "No."

And he had people scratching their heads when he said in a political speech:

Half the lies our opponents tell about us are not true.

Because of the frequency and magnificence of his verbal blunders, Roche became a legend in his own time. As a result, numerous cockamamie sayings were attributed to him, even though his opponents undoubtedly created some of them. Here's a sampler of Roche's verbal misadventures:

Happy are the parents that have no children.

**While I write this letter, I have a pistol in one hand
and a sword in the other.**

**Little children who could neither walk nor talk
were running about in the streets cursing their Maker.**

The cup of our trouble is running over, but, alas, is not yet full.

In twentieth-century America, Samuel Goldwyn became famous for his verbal gaffes. Born in Poland in 1879, the orphaned Goldwyn immigrated to England at age twelve, and three years later to the United States. He spoke Yiddish and Polish until moving to England, when he began his lifelong struggle with the intricacies—and especially the idioms—of the English language. The producer of such classic films as *The Best Years of Our Lives* and *Wuthering Heights*, he's now better known for his fractured English. While many of his remarks had to do with the mixing of metaphors ("Keep a stiff upper chin" or "Take the bull by the teeth"), many were wonderfully oxymoronic:

Our comedies are not to be laughed at.

Gentlemen, include me out.

I don't think anybody should write his autobiography until after he's dead.

He's living beyond his means, but he can afford it.

If I could drop dead right now, I'd be the happiest man alive.

Whereas Goldwyn's inadvertent remarks in his earlier years were genuine, as he grew older and became famous for what became known as "Goldwynisms" he deliberately cultivated them, often relying on his talented staff of screenwriters and publicists for assistance.

Another Hollywood legend noted for inadvertent creations was Michael Curtiz. The director of more than 120 films, including *Casablanca,* the Hungarian-born Curtiz spoke a broken English that resulted in some hilarious misstatements.

Could you get a little closer apart?
DIRECTING TWO STARS IN A LOVE SCENE

Now ride off in all directions.
DIRECTING THE HORSEBACK-RIDING GARY COOPER

Separate together in a bunch.

It's impossible to talk about inadvertent oxymoronica without discussing Lawrence Peter "Yogi" Berra, the catcher for the New York Yankees from the late 1940s to the early 1960s. An exceptional ballplayer, he was the American League's Most Valuable Player three times. After retiring, he managed the New York Yankees and the New York Mets, never quite achieving the success as a manager that he had enjoyed as a ballplayer. During his career, Yogi delighted players, writers, and fans with his unique way of expressing himself. His colorful locutions, known as "Yogi-isms" or "Berraisms," were widely reported in the press. In a 1961 World Series game in Yankee Stadium, Berra was charged with an error when, blinded by the late afternoon sun, he dropped a fly ball. After the game, he explained to writers:

It gets late early out there.

As with Sam Goldwyn and Sir Boyle Roche, Yogi's verbal blunders included mangled metaphors, scrambled syntax, and memorable malapropisms (which we won't consider here). But there were a host of oxymoronic observations as well:

Ninety percent of this game is half mental.

Always go to other people's funerals,
otherwise they won't come to yours.

Nothing is like it seems, but everything is exactly like it is.

It's tough to make predictions, especially about the future.

I didn't say everything I said.

Other examples of inadvertent oxymoronica aren't so funny. For a time in the 1990s, Washington, D.C. was referred to as "the Murder Capital of the United States" because it had the highest homicide rate in the country. Attempting to deal with the city's public relations problems, then-mayor Marion Barry said to reporters:

> **Outside of the killings, Washington has
> one of the lowest crime rates in the country.**

Barry was not the only Washington politician capable of such tortured logic. At about the same time, a D.C. city councilman named John Bowman observed:

> **If crime went down 100 percent,
> it would still be fifty times higher than it should be.**

Some examples of inadvertent oxymoronica are downright idiotic. A classic example emerged during the Vietnam War. Just after the village of Ben Tre was demolished by American bombs and rockets in 1968, an Associated Press report quoted an anonymous U. S. Major as saying:

> **It became necessary to destroy the town to save it.**

After the remark was published, many observers pointed out that this kind of thinking was the reason "military intelligence" was so often considered a contradiction in terms.

Another example occurred a few years ago in Kenya, when a gang of boys at a boarding school raided a girls' dormitory, raping seventy-one girls and killing nineteen. Defying comprehension, the deputy principal of the school said:

> **The boys never meant any harm against the girls.**
> **They just meant to rape.**

Whether hilarious or horrendous, all inadvertent oxymoronic remarks are verbal blunders that make a very specific type of mistake—they contain an internal contradiction or incongruity that is not obvious to the speaker. In the remainder of this chapter, we'll look at a few dozen more.

> **Exposure to dioxin . . . is usually not disabling but may be fatal.**
> ANONYMOUS, IN A DOW CHEMICAL COMPANY REPORT

> **We find the man who stole the horse not guilty.**
> ANONYMOUS JURY FOREMAN

> **Beware! To touch these wires is instant death.**
> **Anyone found doing so will be prosecuted.**
> ANONYMOUS RAILROAD STATION SIGN

> **I am a great mayor; I am an upstanding Christian man;**
> **I am an intelligent man; I am a deeply educated man;**
> **I am a humble man.**
> MARION BARRY

> **There are two kinds of truth. There are real truths**
> **and there are made-up truths.**
> MARION BARRY, AFTER HIS DRUG ARREST

> **The similarities between me and my father are different.**
> DALE BERRA, YOGI'S SON

Those who survived the San Francisco earthquake said,
"Thank God, I'm still alive."
But, of course, those who died, their lives will never be the same again.

SEN. BARBARA BOXER

I have opinions of my own—strong opinions—
but I don't always agree with them.

GEORGE H. W. BUSH

We're enjoying sluggish times, and not enjoying them very much.

GEORGE H. W. BUSH, DURING THE 1992 RECESSION

People say I'm indecisive, but I don't know about that.

GEORGE H. W. BUSH

I think anybody who doesn't think I'm smart enough
to handle the job is underestimating.

GEORGE W. BUSH

For a century and a half now, America and Japan have formed
one of the great and enduring alliances of modern times.

GEORGE W. BUSH

Presidents, whether things are good or bad,
get the blame. I understand that.

GEORGE W. BUSH

There's no question that the minute I got elected, the storm clouds
on the horizon were getting nearly directly overhead.

GEORGE W. BUSH

One of the common denominators I have found
is that expectations rise above that which is expected.

GEORGE W. BUSH

I've been up and down so many times
that I feel as if I'm in a revolving door.

CHER

When I told the people of Northern Ireland that I was an atheist,
a woman in the audience stood up and said,
"Yes, but is it the God of the Catholics or the God of the Protestants
in whom you don't believe?"

QUENTIN CRISP

He had a God-given killer instinct.

AL DAVIS, NFL COACH, ON GEORGE BLANDA

A billion here, a billion there, and pretty soon
you're talking about real money.

SEN. EVERETT DIRKSEN, ON WASHINGTON, D.C.

FISCAL POLICY

If Lincoln were alive today, he'd roll over in his grave.

GERALD FORD

Nolan Ryan is pitching much better
now that he has his curve ball straightened out.

JOE GARAGIOLA

Capital punishment is our society's recognition
of the sanctity of human life.

SEN. ORRIN HATCH, ARGUING FOR THE DEATH PENALTY

IN DRUG CRIME MURDERS

If one is willing to have children,
rhythm is probably the best method of contraception.

ELIZABETH HAWES

Democracy used to be a good thing,
but it has now got into the wrong hands.

SEN. JESSE HELMS

It's funny the way most people love the dead.
Once you are dead, you are made for life.

JIMI HENDRIX

The sky's the limit if you have a roof over your head.

SOL HUROK

Elevate those guns a little lower.

ANDREW JACKSON, AT BATTLE OF MOBILE IN 1815

For the first time in history, profits are higher than ever before.

LYNDON JOHNSON

I think the free-enterprise system is absolutely too important
to be left to the voluntary action of the marketplace.

RICHARD KELLY, REPUBLICAN CONGRESSMAN FROM FLORIDA

Some quiet guys are inwardly outgoing.

RALPH KINER

I don't see much of Alfred anymore since he got so interested in sex.

MRS. ALFRED KINSEY

The best thing is to look natural,
but it takes makeup to look natural.

CALVIN KLEIN

If you are killed because you are a writer,
that's the maximum expression of respect, you know.

MARIO VARGAS LLOSA

That's the most unheard-of thing I ever heard of.

SEN. JOSEPH MCCARTHY, ON A WITNESS'S TESTIMONY

A man can have two, maybe three love affairs
while he's married. After that, it's cheating.

YVES MONTAND

We should respect Mexico's right to chart its own independent course,
provided the course is not antagonistic to our interests.

RICHARD NIXON

And now a record by Glenn Miller, who became
a legend in his own time by his untimely death.

NICHOLAS PARSONS, ON A BBC RADIO BROADCAST

You call this a script? Give me
a couple of $5,000-a-week writers and I'll write it myself.

JOSEPH PASTERNAK

I don't know anything about music. In my line you don't have to.

ELVIS PRESLEY

I believe we are on an irreversible trend toward
more freedom and democracy. But that could change.

DAN QUAYLE

I don't want to tell you any half-truths
unless they're completely accurate.

DENNIS RAPPAPORT, BOXING MANAGER

If you could add together the power of prayer of the people
just in this room, what would be its megatonnage?

RONALD REAGAN, DURING A PRAYER BREAKFAST

The late F. W. H. Myers used to tell
how he asked a man at a dinner table
what he thought would happen to him when he died.
The man tried to ignore the question, but, on being pressed, replied,
"Oh well, I suppose I shall inherit eternal bliss,
but I wish you wouldn't talk about such unpleasant subjects."

BERTRAND RUSSELL

The atomic bomb is a marvelous gift
that was given to us by a wise God.

PHYLLIS SCHLAFLY

The team has come along slow but fast.

CASEY STENGEL, ON THE 1969 NEW YORK METS

If this thing starts to snowball,
it will catch fire right across the country.

ROBERT THOMPSON, CANADIAN POLITICIAN

Index